Turning to Birds

The Power and Beauty of Noticing

Lili Taylor

CROWN
NEW YORK

CROWN
An imprint of the Crown Publishing Group
A division of Penguin Random House LLC
1745 Broadway
New York, NY 10019
crownpublishing.com
penguinrandomhouse.com

2026 Crown Trade Paperback Edition

Illustrations by Anna Koska; watercolor background on title page, Contents page, and chapter openers by Shutterstock / Improviser

Library of Congress Cataloging-in-Publication Data is on file with the publisher.

ISBN 978-0-593-72859-8
Ebook ISBN 978-0-593-72858-1

Originally published in hardcover in slightly different form in the United States by Crown, an imprint of the Crown Publishing Group, a division of Penguin Random House LLC, in 2025.

Editors: Libby Burton and Matt Inman
Editorial Assistants: Brittany Bailey and Fariza Hawke
Production editors: Terry Deal and Isabella Franco
Text designer: Aubrey Khan
Production: Heather Williamson and Alison Kaitcer
Copy editor: Elisabeth Magnus
Proofreaders: Tracy R. Lynch and Miriam Taveras
Publicists: Mary Moates, Bree Martinez, and Gwyneth Stansfield
Marketers: Kimberly Lew and Hannah Perrin

Manufactured in the United States of America

2nd Printing

First Paperback Edition

The authorized representative in the EU for product safety and compliance is Penguin Random House Ireland, Morrison Chambers, 32 Nassau Street, Dublin D02 YH68, Ireland, https://eu-contact.penguin.ie.

For Mom

Contents

Turning to Birds

1

Introduction: In the Beginning

We all know what a bird is. They live in our yards, in our cities, on our seas. They exist on every single continent. They are the subject of children's books and books for grown-ups. They are depicted in visual art, in television documentaries, in movies. They have been around for more than 145 million years. One of the earliest cave paintings was of a bird. We use them as symbols and metaphors. We even eat them.

But most people don't really know birds—or rather, they aren't *aware* of them. I used to be one of those people. I knew birds existed. I thought about them, maybe even more than the average person. But I didn't know them.

There's a term in the birding world for the bird who brings one into the world of birding. That term is *spark bird.* And I don't have one. I wish I did. I get asked the question all the time, and it's one of those answers that could be perfect for an interview: clean, concise, and easy. But my memory dims when I try to recall which bird first opened my heart and mind to all birds. Class Aves, phylum Chordata, belonging to the kingdom

Animalia, categorized under Reptilia (but because their blood is warm, they are not reptiles). Birds are technically flying dinosaurs. And I love them.

I started to sense birds in a deeper way about fifteen years ago, when I took an emotional sabbatical from my work as an actor. I'd been going from project to project without a break and felt depleted, so I retreated to my house in upstate New York, about two hours from New York City. The house sits on one hundred acres of working farmland. When I bought the property, I signed an agricultural conservation easement with Scenic Hudson, the environmental organization dedicated to safeguarding the Hudson Valley's landscapes—including the region's farmland. It's a way of ensuring that farmland will be kept open and available for agricultural use. There are several agricultural easements in the surrounding area, with a local farmer, Kenny Migliorelli, farming on most of them. I've become friends with Kenny and learned how stressful it is to be a farmer. There is so little in his control, and it changes day to day. Small farmers are probably closer than most people to the very essence of life.

During the time of my sabbatical, Kenny was letting the fields go fallow, meaning he wasn't cultivating a crop but instead putting in plants that would restore the soil. For the first time since I'd bought the home, there were no big crop-tending or harvesting machines or trucks coming through the property.

And there, in the stillness, I started to hear birds. It was as if I'd switched my audio input from one dimension to Dolby stereo. Birds' sounds began to differentiate themselves from one another. They were no longer generic tweets or chirps but specific sounds, with meaning. There were things going on out in the yard: stories, drama, mating, fighting, death. During that time of personal quiet, I entered a world of sound outside myself—and I've never left.

Now, it's not that my hearing is better than it was; it's that my perception of the world is wider and deeper. This new awareness of the sounds of birds drew me into a parallel universe, one of constant change and movement, full of life and the will to survive. Wherever I am, whenever I listen, I can tap into that profound energy of survival and draw power from it.

Tapping into that power was what gave me the oomph I needed to return to the city from my sabbatical. As I settled back into my life in Brooklyn, I knew that what I'd found on the farm I could find anywhere. It was simply up to me to seek it out.

During the early days of Covid, when everything stopped, I was reminded of that period of quiet—only this time, everyone around me was also experiencing the solitude and silence that I had discovered a dozen years earlier. I heard people talk about looking out their windows as if for the first time and noticing creatures with wings out there. Friends reached out to say that they'd thought of me because they recalled that I liked birds, and they wanted to tell me, "I like them too!" Birds became a news story, a topic of discussion in articles and on podcasts.

The comment that "birds are having a moment" is now

something I hear frequently in the birding community. I serve on the boards of two birding organizations, the National Audubon Society and the New York City Bird Alliance, where there's a new urgency to capitalize on this enthusiasm. We no longer have to spend our energy or resources convincing people that birds are great and can instead find ways we can all work together to protect birds and the places they inhabit.

I'm not surprised that birds are finally having a moment. I've long had a sense that people feel a connection to birds, even if they don't know it. I never thought I'd find a theory to back up this intuition, but I did, in a concept called biophilia. Developed by E. O. Wilson, the eminent biologist best known for his groundbreaking work on ants, the biophilia hypothesis asserts that humans are genetically predisposed to be attracted to nature. According to Wilson, a love for the natural world—and the search for a means to fulfill it—is as basic and instinctual as our needs for food, water, touch, and community.

There is growing scientific evidence supporting the idea that the natural world has an effect on us at once positive, concrete, and profound. A recent study published in the journal *Emotion* examined something called an "awe walk," a stroll during which you intentionally shift your attention outward instead of inward. The article's title reflects this practice's results: "Big Smile, Small Self: Awe Walks Promote Prosocial Positive Emotions in Older Adults." The lead author of the study, neurologist Virginia Sturm, has since commented, "I find it remarkable that the simplest intervention in the world—just a three-minute conversation at the beginning of the study suggesting that participants practice feeling awe on their weekly walks—was able to drive significant shifts in their daily emotional experience. . . . This suggests promoting the experience of awe could be an extremely low-cost tool for improving the emotional health of older adults through a simple shift in mindset."

I've been taking "awe walks" for years, except I call it "birding." So it's possible for me to experience awe every day. All I have to do is remind myself to lift my eyes from the ground and look around me. If I do so, I will find a bird. That's a fact, no matter where I am. I might be on a concrete sidewalk in Manhattan and my eyes will land on a pigeon, and even that pigeon will help me "intentionally shift my attention outward instead of inward." Pigeons are much more interesting than we give them credit for. Stop and observe a pigeon for more than three minutes, and you'll find a story. Here is one I witnessed the other day.

A male pigeon was circling a female pigeon. How did I know it was a male? Do male pigeons look different from females? No, you can't tell them apart based on their plumage or other physical characteristics. But as is the case with most bird species, the male pigeon must convince the female that his genetics are better than those of the other male pigeons pecking at the ground nearby. So this male pigeon puffed his neck feathers out, bobbed his head up and down, and cooed. Then he flew up into the air, slapped his wings above his body, touched down again, and resumed his circling.

As I watched, something about that wing thing struck me; it seemed specific, not random. When I got home, I looked into it. The behavior I witnessed is called "wing clapping," and though it's unusual, pigeons aren't the only birds that do it. The male short-eared owl also wing-claps to impress the female, or to warn off predators. He snaps his wings below his body—instead of above, like a pigeon—in two to six bursts of clapping that some say sound just like applause.

Speaking of applause, I'm an actor, as I mentioned. I bring that up because I've discovered that the most important skill I use in acting I also use when I'm looking at birds. That skill is *listening*—by which I don't mean hearing what another actor is saying or the sound a bird is making. When I'm on stage with a scene partner, I might find myself thinking about what I'm going to eat after the show: *maybe tonight I'll get the steak frites*. Then I'll think that the audience hates me and wants me off the stage, that I should give up acting. My focus flits about, taking in everything except what is right in front of me—which is my scene partner, my fellow actor, who is a source of energy and can provide stimuli that are unique and unknown to me.

How can I focus on them? I make a concerted effort to shut out all that is not my fellow actor. As my focus narrows, it also gets deeper because it's penetrating and intent on the essence contained within a single point: the actor. This is a process that's by default imperfect. My mental chatter continues, my eyes dart here and there, my body moves around the stage, but I'm still capable of simultaneously focusing on the actor. That's the tension, and it's possible to hold it for a finite period of time.

When listening, I arrive at my destination when the object of my focus—whether an actor or a bird, a dragonfly, the rustling leaves of an oak tree—has transformed into a subject with its own singular, authentic being. I'm there. But what exactly is *there*?

Because the phrase "in the moment" has been so over- and misused, we've lost sight of its importance. And that's a shame, because it's a lovely, profound concept about truth and authenticity.

Other names for the quality of inhabiting the moment are being "in the zone" or experiencing "flow." The psychologist Mihaly Csikszentmihalyi popularized the latter term, *flow,* and defined it as such: "The ego falls away. Time flies. Every action, movement, and thought follows inevitably from the previous one, like playing jazz. Your whole being is involved, and you're using your skills to the utmost." Listening is the most important skill that facilitates flow, and because it's a skill it can be learned. As the auditory neuroscientist Seth S. Horowitz writes in *The Universal Sense,* "The difference between the sense of hearing and the skill of listening is attention." When most of my attention is focused on the other, then I can say I am listening. *Attention* is the key.

The Latin root of attention is *tendere,* meaning "to stretch toward, especially with the mind." If I'm paying attention, that means I'm extending beyond my baseline; it wouldn't be a stretch if it was my normal state. I like knowing this because it reminds me that paying attention is not easy. It's uncomfortable. I'll inevitably snap back to my baseline because to hold a stretch is untenable; it would no longer be a stretch if it became static. But I like to think that my starting point shifts each time I pay attention. I've gained something in listening, and I don't return empty-handed. That experience fills me up, adds more to me.

One of the lovely things about being in the zone as an actor is the intrinsic fact that the zone is shared with another, be it a fellow actor or the audience. An actor can't act alone. When I'm in the zone observing a bird, it's a wonderful feeling, but it's private, personal. Yet if I keep paying attention I'll become more and more—"morethanme," to borrow a poetic word from E. E. Cummings.

The philosopher William James, also known as the father of American psychology, wrote that our lives consist of those things that we have attended to. The act of paying attention speaks to one's quality of living. In filling myself up I create meaning, find answers to the questions that can hound me: What are my days like? Did I give it my all? Did I carpe diem? What did I do while I was here?

I don't bound out of bed every morning with the desire to live life to the fullest. In fact, sometimes the first word that comes to mind is *no.* My default impulse is often to turn away from potential experiences for reasons I don't really understand.

I found a maxim attributed to the English biologist and philosopher Herbert Spencer that helps me reckon with this impulse: "There is a principle which is a bar against all information, which is proof against all argument, and which cannot fail to keep a man in everlasting ignorance—that principle is contempt prior to investigation."

Investigation is probably the second most important skill I use for both acting and observing birds. It comes from the Latin *vestigium,* meaning "a footprint"; "to follow the footprints of; to track, hence, to go in search of; to see for oneself." What I like about this definition is its focus on the footprint, the trace, the outline of the thing under investigation—and not the thing itself.

I didn't grasp until many years into my acting life that an actor is really a kind of psychological detective, tracking piece after piece of emotional information. But the information is not the entirety of the thing: it is an outline I must fill in by incorporating the previous pieces of information. Acting requires a loose focus, two contradictory states—and is thus difficult to hold. So it's all the more gratifying, after searching, observing, tracking, when I reach her, the character.

If an actor were to pledge an oath, it would be this: I will do my utmost to understand the character as she is. I will examine the script thoroughly so that I have a deep and empathetic understanding of her situation. And when I bring that preparation to bear on the stage or in front of the camera, my aim is to seek the truth, then transmit it via a cluster of emotions to my fellow human beings who bear witness on the other side.

Why is all of this important? And what do birds have to do with it? It's hard to have contempt when you're looking at a bird. It's hard *not* to be inspired to investigate when looking at a bird. In following birds, I have discovered insects, trees, plants, radar, navigation, drawing, painting, oceans, deserts, forests, and people. In essence, the world.

There are many reasons for birds' unique standing in our animal kingdom: of course, they fly, but just as significantly, they get around. The majority of bird species don't stay in the same location all year but spend half their time in a totally different place; for instance, gray-crowned rosy finches can spend summer as far north as Alaska and the Yukon, and winter as far south as New Mexico. They must flourish in both places, or else they die. They erase the human-made boundaries cutting through the planet and instead reveal an interconnected, complex system that operates as a whole. They tell us what is going on in the world.

Birds tell us.

I didn't come up with that phrase; the National Audubon Society did. The Society is dedicated to helping birds and the places they need to thrive. I love being on the board; on a superficial level, it gives me some solid cred. I've inspired many an impressed, raised eyebrow when I mention my role in the organization. "You? You're on the board?" Yep, you heard that right. The actor was invited to sit with the grown-ups.

Most board members are high-performing, well-educated, highly intelligent, and engaged members of society. During some board meetings, I have no idea what they're talking about. I didn't know "development" meant raising money; in my profession, it means that people are working on creating a script.

Recently, our organization supported an exhaustive study, published in *Science* and covered on the front page of *The New York Times,* that concluded that the United States and Canada have lost three billion birds over the last fifty years. The situation was far worse than most scientists and birding enthusiasts had realized. But the study presents solid data that shows us where and what the problems are, which is a crucial step in building toward solutions.

Now, why should someone be interested in a book about birds by an actor, Audubon board member though she may be? Well, I'm not any actor; I'm me. Sanford Meisner, the wonderful acting teacher, whom I've never met but whose book *Sanford Meisner on Acting* I've read like a bible, said over and over again that there is no one like you, and you have to use you: your acting will not be good until it is only yours. That's true of music, acting, anything creative. You work until, finally, nobody is acting like *you*.

It's taken me years to embrace the concept of using myself in acting, but that's a story for another book. Meisner also said, "It takes at least twenty years to learn how to act." If he's to be believed, then I'm just about on time.

In the simplest terms, I want to share what I see and hear, specifically in regard to birds and acting, with you, the reader. I think the two are connected in important ways that illuminate something bigger about who we are and how we can be in the world.

If I were to draw a Venn diagram linking the subjects of acting and birding, here are the skills they would share:

Listening
Attention
Investigation
Observation
Perception
Specificity

These are some of the things I do when I'm acting and when I'm looking at birds. They are skills that require effort and practice, and they can be developed. Diving into the linguistic origins of these six skills reveals a complex set of connections, like some underground network of fungi. But, like any cooperative system, they share a common principle: they are all different ways of coming to know something.

I've talked about the roots of listening, attention, and investigation and how they are relevant to both acting and birding. But how do the other three skills enter the picture?

Observation is "an instance of watching attentively." The word *observe* has associations with religious rites, and there is something elevated about approaching a being or object and watching it with focus. As with investigation, the word *follow* is often included in the meaning of observation—you follow something because you care and want to know. You don't drop it. You attend to it and commit.

I've been playing with the concept of observation since I started acting classes in my early teens. Actors are taught to observe people. It's one of the first exercises we're given: observe an animal at the zoo; observe a person sitting on a bench in a park. I understood the impetus behind the assignment, but it always felt a bit forced to me. The end result had more to do with how I was going to use an observation, and I don't want to stare at another human being so I can pocket some eccentric characteristic to use for "my acting" someday. True observation is a more generous act, in that you make room for the other by clearing away motives and assumptions so you can take it in its totality.

Perception, the act of perceiving. The Latin root there is *capere,* "to grasp." It even says in the dictionary, "literally, to take in entirely." That's what I'm trying to do when I'm working with a character: to grasp her situation, her reality. "To become aware of, to know by means of the senses, to recognize, to discern"—these words guide me like some sort of tactical spelunker, giving me the gear with which to explore the depths of a soul. When I'm birding, these principles lift me out of myself and toward the bird I'm hoping to know.

The root of *specificity* is *species,* "a kind of"—but what's cool is there's another root in there, *ficus* or *facere,* "to make." Perhaps listening and specificity lie at the two ends of a pole and in between lies the process of making—of emptying out, taking in, grasping, noticing, knowing until the other is its own special kind of thing.

Specificity, like *observation,* is a word deeply embedded in acting pedagogy. Another class I attended was taught by the actor Kent Gash, who said, "General is the death of acting. Specific. You have to make it specific." And then he actually yelled, "Specificity! Specificity!" at me. And I heard him.

Why is specificity so important in acting—and, even more importantly, in life? When I'm working to make some situation in a character's life specific, I'm attempting to grant the whole experience significance. Getting the details right shows that I care about being here, I care about my work, and I care how it affects others. Human nature can smell a rat. We know when something is superficial, general, a throwaway. Our survival depends on stories that connect us to a deeper part of ourselves and others. Access to that depth requires care and work.

Now, amid all this highfalutin talk about my principles, there is another truth: I'm really lazy. I could sit and look out a window all day. I made a sitting perch by the window in the back of my apartment in Brooklyn. The other day, I looked down and watched a squirrel dig up the new grass seed I planted. Oh well. The house sparrows—those are the little brown birds that aren't pigeons that you see all over the city—

fly in and land around the feeder. I start counting them, and then wonder why I'm counting them. I tell myself it's important to know if the numbers vary day to day. Is it still around twenty? I tell myself that I'd just like to look at them and not have to count. I look up at a cloud. I try to see if I can identify and name it, but then I let it go because right now, I just need to look at a frigging cloud without lifting a finger. Just looking at the clouds for the sake of looking at the clouds is a kind of play. And I need to play.

Mihaly Csikszentmihalyi, the psychologist who coined the definition of *flow,* dedicated his career to the study of play. He did so for two reasons: because the subject of play related to another of his areas of interest—creativity—and because he felt confident that play is among the most positive experiences in life. Over time, he realized play was what the Greeks called an *autotelic activity,* meaning the whole purpose of the activity is the experience itself. He became convinced that an experience "is worth having for its own sake."

I didn't know that a word existed to describe "experience for experience's sake." The concept of an autotelic activity liberates me from feeling there must be a result from an experience—something to show for it, something I can use someday. I don't have to kill two birds with one stone to get the most out of that stone and my time. Instead, I can forgo the stone and just kill time experiencing the bird.

And that brings me back to this book.

You remember those invisible ink coloring books from your

childhood? The pages look blank but for the faint outlines of a few objects: a landscape with grass, a tree, the sky. But once the magic pen connects with the special paper, a chemical reaction occurs, and objects that were invisible begin to appear. You draw long enough on the picture and a whole world reveals itself. I hope you, reader, feel the same surprise and delight that a kid feels when those invisible objects—in this case, birds—emerge, through stories and observations, recollections, and encounters.

As I said, I try to think of myself as an ambassador for birds. It would be a moral failure on my part not to share what I've gleaned from them. One thing I've learned by watching birds is that there's always a story. If you stay a few more moments than you'd prefer to, if you resist the urge to move on, get going, get busy, look at your phone—if you just keep watching the bird, that's when it happens. The *it* is simply life: experiencing, imagining, feeling, breathing, sharing. Then you move on, and the bird moves on, but you have a new moment to connect with your other moments. And at the end of the day, that's all we have: a life of moments, assembled as one.

The other day I reread this quote I had saved and burst into tears:

> If there is a heaven, and I am allowed entrance, I will ask for no more than an endless living world to walk through and explore. I will carry with me an inexhaustible supply of notebooks, from which I can send back reports to the

> more sedentary spirits (mostly molecular and cell biologists). Along the way I would expect to meet kindred spirits.

In saving the passage when I first encountered it, I knew it was from the introduction to the book *Field Notes on Science and Nature,* but I didn't know who its author was. I wasn't surprised when I discovered these were the words of E. O. Wilson, the biologist who named the concept of biophilia. I smiled at the discovery. My scattered collections of scraps of meaning coalesced, forming a network of connections. Satellites that had heretofore seemed orphaned in space were now part of something greater: they orbited within a value system, a circle that was big enough to contain many circles of meaning, intersecting, connecting, always in potentia.

I don't believe in heaven. I don't know what happens when we die, and I don't spend much time thinking about it. It overwhelms me. But when I think about being here, I realize I'm allowed entrance to this earth right now, even though I don't always feel like I belong. I'm alive. I'm here. I want to make the most of it. And I want to share my reports of this endless living world with my kindred spirits.

2

Bird Festival

I'm in a cab on the Brooklyn-Queens Expressway, just before dawn, sky deep blue. I'm heading to LaGuardia Airport, and I'm going somewhere I've never been before: a bird festival.

I didn't know such a thing existed. I was a recent entrant into the world of birds; it was still foreign, in the true sense of the word, meaning a place situated on the outside, beyond. As a newcomer in a new world, I was processing new concepts daily, new words and images totally outside my lexicon, my consciousness.

I had only recently learned that I could look for birds beyond my backyard. That discovery brought me to Central Park, a park I loved and often visited but never to specifically look for birds. And it was there that I overheard a group of birders talking about a bird festival. The phrase activated neuron activity for me, forming into a pleasant mind map of associations: birds, festival, celebration, me, go, possible, no, maybe, *yes*.

Typing "bird festival" into Google transported me gently

into this new reality. The first page assured me that, yes, they really exist: "A great way to enjoy bird watching is by going to festivals." The second page drew my attention to where and when this could happen: the Rio Grande Valley Birding Festival in Harlingen, Texas; the Space Coast Birding and Wildlife Festival in Cape Canaveral, Florida; the Hawk Weekend Festival in Duluth, Minnesota; the Potholes and Prairies Birding Festival in Bismarck, North Dakota. The search got better with each page, which had never happened to me before.

Someday, I would like to stand in front of a map that identifies every bird festival in the world, close my eyes, circle my pointer finger over the map, and let it swoop down and land, que sera, sera style. For my first outing, though, I needed to find a festival close-ish to home and one that fell around Mother's Day, which made it easier to justify to myself and my family why Mama was leaving to go see birds.

Back in the cab, the new sun brightens the vehicle with golden light; even the narrow, pockmarked concrete of the BQE looks beautiful. Time opens up and holds me.

I'm jolted out of this reverie when the cabbie says, "Where are you going?"

"Oh, ah, I'm going to Ohio."

"Oh yeah, what's in Ohio?"

"Oh, ah, just a festival."

"What kind of festival?"

"Birds. A bird festival."

"Birds?"

"Yeah, birds."

There's a short beat before he says, "Birds."

I think to myself, should I just fucking say it? I'm going to say it.

"I'm a birder."

"A birder?"

"Yeah, I'm a birder. I like birds."

"Oh."

Silence. And that's okay. It doesn't matter what he thinks. I said it. I'm committed. I'm a birder, goddammit.

"You know, my aunt loves birds," he says, then pauses for a moment. His eyes meet mine in the rearview mirror. He looks back to the road, then back to the mirror. "That's nice. So, you're going there to see birds."

"Yes!"

I land in the Detroit airport and hop on the shuttle bus to the rental car lot. The driver is a friendly Detroit native. He's got the radio on; R&B fills the bus. He asks me where I'm going.

"I'm going to a bird festival," I say, with more conviction this time.

"A bird festival?! Well, goddamn. What do you do at a bird festival?"

"I have no idea. But I like birds and I'm going."

"Well, goddamn. That's all right. That's cool. Hmmm. Birds. What do you know? Birds are all right."

I pick up the rental car and set out for Maumee Bay Lodge

and Conference Center in Oregon, Ohio, about an hour-and-a-half drive through mostly farmland. Having grown up in Illinois, I'm familiar with this landscape, the flat expanse of crops. But I have no idea what birds will be here.

The Maumee Bay Lodge, located within Maumee Bay State Park. It's got an old-school feel to it, by which I mean it was built in the '70s. There's an expansive lobby with large chairs and beige wood tables, and a restaurant with nice waitresses who wear brown synthetic uniforms and, it seems, have worked there for twenty years. Tacky chandeliers cast light onto the loopy patterned carpet. The place isn't too stuck in the past, but it hasn't quite caught up to the present either.

It's also a conference center and, right now, the site of "the Biggest Week in American Birding," so named because it coincides with the peak of songbird migration. At the entrance are two rectangular folding tables with name tags laid out. Volunteer staff, mostly older women, oversee the tables and greet me as I walk in. They let me know that it's very important that I get my name tag and, of course, my Biggest Week in American Birding black canvas tote bag, which contains a notebook and pen, stickers, a cup, coupons, a brochure about the weekend, and a checklist of all the birds I might come across during the festival. This region of northwestern Ohio has another name, the women tell me: the "Warbler Capital of the World."

In the United States and Canada, there are about fifty-four different species of warblers. Most of them spend their winters in Mexico or Central or South America, migrate north in

April and May to breed, then head back south starting around August.

Birds follow migratory routes, called flyways, which are like superhighways in the sky. There are four major flyways in North America: the Pacific, Central, Mississippi, and Atlantic flyways. This festival is located at the convergence of the Mississippi and Atlantic flyways. It's on one of the Great Lakes, Lake Erie—from a bird's point of view, the first large body of water since the Atlantic or the Gulf of Mexico, but totally different because it's freshwater. From here, many of the warblers will go on to the Canadian boreal forest to breed, way up in the Northern Hemisphere, but this place is the perfect pit stop, with fresh water, food, and shelter until the next leg of the journey.

I leave the nice ladies and enter the lobby populated with mostly older people wearing beige, binoculars around their necks, name tags on their beige jackets. As I drift through the crowd, more diversity pops: a teenage birder with a father; a guy in black with dyed black hair, a subtle goth birder; a small group of teenagers moving quickly through the crowd to get outside.

I drift toward an area of cloth-covered folding tables at the edge of the lobby, displaying all aspects of the birding world: bird books, bird-nest boxes, bird sculptures, bird paintings, clothes with birds, bird jewelry, bird tour guide information, bird activist literature, optics, bird gear.

I want everything. I remind myself that I'll be here for a few days; I have time to take in these sumptuous tables. But, oh, the books. All around are books about birds that I've never seen, very specific books with specific titles: *Owls by Day and Night, Bird Tracks and Signs, The Birds of Eastern Ohio.*

I can get caught up in paraphernalia, sometimes more so than the subject of the paraphernalia itself. But I came to Ohio to see birds, so I should do that before I spend the whole day inside buying things related to them. I reluctantly step back into the lobby, returning to the friendly older women at the registration tables. I ask them where the action is, and they say: the boardwalk on Magee Marsh.

On the drive to Magee Marsh, I don't see any birds. As I drive through the farmland, I work on trusting, to counter the doubt creeping in. Maybe there's a small park in the middle of this farmland with some birds? I'm not feeling encouraged by the sameness, the flatness. I turn off Country Route 2 onto a long, winding road lined with trees. And my doubt fades away as the trees open to reveal marshland and Lake Erie beyond.

In front of the lake is a long parking lot packed with cars. I see birders everywhere, a Richard Scarry cartoon of birders: some in groups, some alone, couples, Amish birders, birders in wheelchairs, children looking for birds. And this is just the parking lot. But birds don't care about boundaries: if there's a food source in the parking lot, then the birds will be there, and the birders with them.

The boardwalk is about a mile long in a seven-acre woodlot, boasting a variety of different habitats along its length, some of which play host to specific species of birds. Numbers are carved into fence posts about every two hundred feet, twenty in all. The numbers correlate to a site with a name: 17 is Big Tree Corner, 20 is Scrub Line, 7 is Tower.

It's 2:00 p.m. when I enter the Boardwalk West Entrance: wooden planks, wood guardrails on either side, topped with a six-inch-wide board on top, allowing people to lean over and rest their elbows as they look at birds.

Some birders stand at the railings; others keep moving slowly along the boardwalk, passing each other like two opposing teams after a game, except no one lost. I move along 'cause that's what I do when I don't know what I'm doing—I keep moving. I stop next to a small group focused on a bird midway up a tree.

I can stop next to strangers, look at what they are looking at, and not feel weird. I can even ask, "What do you see?" And they answer: yellow warbler. I look for the yellow warbler. The small group moves on just as I catch a flash of yellow. They don't say goodbye and don't have to. I stay by myself. That also doesn't feel weird. I want to find the yellow warbler. It's hard searching for a moving thing through the small lens of my binoculars. I lose where I am, like a kid spinning round and round. I'm still a novice with binoculars. Using them is a skill; it takes practice.

The yellow warbler has moved on. I didn't get a good look, only a flash. That's okay. I move on, my shoulders relaxing, the world feeling bigger, as I take in the fact that I have no schedule, that I can do what I want, when I want. I have the freedom to follow the rhythm of the birds, the people. I can let go and flow.

There's a large group ahead of me: a cluster of more than fifteen, five people deep, focused in the same direction. I pick up my pace, wanting to join.

As I approach, I hear whispers.

"Blackburnian."

"Where?"

"There."

"Do you have him?"

"Where is . . ."

"Oh, I got him. Oh my God, what a beauty."

"Oh, my goodness . . ."

"What is it?"

"A Blackburnian."

An older woman looks at me and smiles. She says, "Isn't that the most beautiful orange you've ever seen?"

But I can't find the bird. The boardwalk has volunteer guides who spot the birds and help others get to them. One volunteer is giving the group a play-by-play of the bird's movements. An old lady says she can't see him. He says, "Think of the tree as a big clock. Right now, the Blackburnian is near three o'clock, moving down . . ."

The guide catapults me toward the bird, as if I'm standing on a knee and he's hoisting me up into the world of a black bird with a fiery orange neck, gleaning the vernal leaves for insects.

Someone else is next to me now. It's a man, who takes his binoculars down, looks at me, and smiles.

"It's something, isn't it?"

"Yes. I've never seen one before."

"Oh! You have a lifer!"

I don't know what a lifer is, but I love the sound of it.

The winds from the south have brought this bird from Colombia on his way north to Canada, where he will breed. The Blackburnian warbler is roughly four inches tall and weighs about 0.35 ounces, though this one probably weighs much less at the moment because he's flown over two thousand miles and has been using muscle fat for fuel. I know it's a "he" because of that fiery orange-red throat that fades into a belly of yellow, jet-black wings dabbed with some white. The female is much more toned down, with no fiery orange or jet black; instead, she's got a pale-yellow neck and drab olive wings.

I can't take my eyes off the orange. The Blackburnian continues flitting deftly around the branches of a tree, gobbling up insects from the leaves—a feast for the hungry. All along the boardwalk were hundreds of starving, exhausted warblers, shining through the trees like gems. The bird lovers crowd the boardwalk, eyes bright and mouths open in awe, softly oohing and ahhhing at the fireworks of warblers.

I stay there until 7:00 p.m. because I can. I thought I would have to leave but then remembered that I could stay.

I can stay with the birds and marvel. I can wander, saunter, run, stand still, alone, in a group.

I'm no longer a foreigner. The world of birds is not outside me. I'm in it.

3

Bins

I see the blue jay with my naked eye. It's about thirty feet away, meaning it's close enough that I can observe its color pattern, beak, and eyes. I can even make out a number of finer details: the punk-rock mohawk of feathers on top of its head, the black feather necklace, and the long blue tail with black stripes.

But now I raise my Swarovski SLC 10x42 binoculars to my eyes. The blue jay is magnified.

It is magnificent. *Magnifico. Magnificare.*

The bird appears larger in my field of vision, but that's not what's magnificent here.

Bigger isn't better. The revelation afforded by the binoculars is the minutiae. There are at least six shades of blue in its plumage; I had no idea that "blue" could contain such a range. At the top of its primary feathers, two rows of small squares are laid like tiles in a mosaic: the top row a sun-filled sky blue, and below a before-dark cobalt. The tiles explode as the blue jay quickly cuts out of my frame.

I lower the binoculars—or "bins," as birders like to call

them. The world zooms back to normal. It's as if I took a trip to another country and am now arriving back in familiar territory, but where is the blue jay? I find it with my naked eye, on the branch of a craggy silver maple.

I bring the bins up to my eyes and descend back into the world of blue, but now I see gray, the shade you see in the sky when it's tornado weather. The gray feathers blend into a jagged black chain draped low over its chest. The brown marble eye blinks, and this time I move with the blue jay as it flies off. My field of vision jumps and shudders as I track it, as if I'm on a boat amid choppy waves, but I keep the bird in view. It lands on the edge of the feeder, a wooden tray filled with black sunflower seeds that rests six feet from the ground atop a pole.

The blue jay dips its giant head into the tray and roughly plucks one seed up in its beak, props the seed between its claws and smashes down with its beak once, twice, three times. It picks into the fractured shell and tosses the heart of the seed back like a shot of whiskey. Then, it bolts out of frame once more. This time I don't follow; I feel like I've eaten that seed too and need a moment to digest.

I BELIEVE BINOCULARS are a worthy investment, even if you're not going to make birding a regular hobby. Along with looking at birds, I use mine to observe:

Bark and leaves on a tree
Butterflies and dragonflies
Ships at sea
Sunlight dancing with the water
Craters on the moon
The Pleiades star cluster
The tragedy that plays out between two different species of ants in New Mexico

THE TWO MAIN types of magnifications used in the birding community are 8x42 and 10x42. The first number indicates how many times the object is magnified beyond our twenty-twenty vision, and the second number stands for the size of the objective lens—the diameter of the lens that is closest to the object you're viewing.

My choice, 10x42s, makes things appear ten times larger. I tried 8x42s for a while, but they didn't transport me. And that's what I'm looking for: by way of the magnification, I'm looking to merge with the bird.

In transporting me beyond the limits of twenty-twenty vision, binoculars facilitate an experience outside reality. I don't do drugs; I do bins. They are, literally and figuratively, a new way of seeing. When I zoom in on a bird, I find myself closer to what it's experiencing; the bins cultivate empathy. Through magnification and specificity, I come to understand a bird's point of view.

❦

My first real bins were Nikon Monarch 8x42s. As I said, I've come to prefer 10x42s, but if you can spend over a hundred dollars and don't want to go over five hundred, that's the pair to get.

There's an incredible range of bins; the two brands at the highest price point, Swarovski and Zeiss, can cost over two thousand dollars, easy. I graduated to Swarovskis, but I must admit that's because they were given to me. I met Swarovski's sales rep, Clay, at the Biggest Week in American Birding Festival, and by the end of the week he asked if I wanted a pair of bins. I told him I couldn't do much for Swarovski because I'm not that kind of celebrity—I'm more of a working actor whom some people know—but I would be more than happy to do whatever I could for him. Clay placed a pair of Swarovski SLC 10x42s in my hands, and I brought them up to my eyes. They struck me as a work of art: a marvel of design, craftsmanship, and technical expertise. What can I say? They're made by a company that cuts diamonds. One day, I left my Swarovskis on the top of the car and drove away. When I returned to find them, they were gone. Lucky for someone else. Having been spoiled by the superior glass, I knew there was no turning back—though for my next pair I tried the other fancy brand, Zeiss, and they were just as magnificent as the Swarovskis.

I try to take my bins with me wherever I go, even in the city. When you wear them out and about in New York, people throw you a second glance: "Wait, that's not a camera. What the . . . Why the hell does that lady have binoculars?"

Of course, you need to be careful using bins in the city, particularly inside, as I often do when I'm looking out my window in Brooklyn. I try to indicate to my neighbors that the bins are only for looking at birds and I would never violate their personal space, but I can't hang a banner out my window saying, "I'm a birder, not a creep!" So I only use the binoculars pointed totally down toward the backyard or totally up to the sky. I never hold them at midrange.

Once there was a Cooper's hawk on the fire escape directly across from my window, at eye level. The Cooper's is a medium-size hawk, meaning it's bigger than a crow and smaller than an eagle. It's a member of the genus *Accipiter,* whereas the red-tailed hawk (a common hawk through the United States; you often see them along highways, perched on telephone poles) is a member of the genus *Buteo. Accipiters* are more agile than *Buteos*—think Tom Cruise in *Top Gun,* flying in and out of narrow granite passageways. I've seen footage from a GoPro camera strapped to the chest of a Cooper's hawk as it navigated a dense forest, and I screamed in delight and terror. A birding friend told me that the Cooper's hawk is comparable to the velociraptor: every other bird is scared to death of them.

This particular Cooper's hawk on the fire escape was surveying the pigeons in my backyard. I try to make room for the whole food chain back there by always putting out seed, though the Cooper's doesn't eat the seed; it eats the pigeons who eat the seed. With the Cooper's perched across from me in front of the neighbor's window, I was itching to pick up my bins, but I simply couldn't do it. That's just not okay—it's like barging through a stranger's door, invading their space and security. Even if I had a hat on that said BIRDER, it wouldn't matter. It's a nonnegotiable for me.

I'VE DISCOVERED SOMETHING interesting about the act of looking up. Try this experiment when you're next out on the street—no bins required. Stand on the sidewalk, look up, and stay looking up for a good couple of minutes. I guarantee you a fellow human walking by will pass you, pause, and then look up too. I don't know where it comes from, this instinct to look up when another human is looking up. Is it from the way, way old days when scary creatures jumped down on us from the tree branches above? But things don't fall from the sky often enough anymore to justify that reaction.

I don't wait for a passerby to ask me what I'm looking at. I tell them: "I'm looking at four blue jays in that tree. They're upset about something. I'm not sure what." And we stand together observing the blue jays, both of us trying to understand what's going on.

One day I was looking at a downy woodpecker on Warren Street between Court and Smith, in Brooklyn. I'm always pleasantly surprised when I see a woodpecker on a regular city street. Woodpeckers need trees—and not just live trees but dead trees as well, which contain a complex ecosystem full of food and nesting spots. I imagine the city can't leave dead trees standing because of the danger of them falling.

I've found woodpeckers challenging to locate because they circle around the trunk of the tree or branch looking for food; often they're either out of sight or in one place digging. So I was very focused on that woodpecker, and my behavior caught the attention of a woman who was coming down the sidewalk from the opposite direction. She was nicely dressed and carrying an umbrella even though rain wasn't in the forecast.

I noticed as her walk went from smooth to halting. She was in. With no hesitation, I said, "I'm looking at a downy woodpecker."

"A what?"

"A downy woodpecker. A bird. Do you know what a woodpecker is?"

"A woodpecker?"

"Yeah . . ." And then the downy suddenly flew to a tree in the yard of a brownstone in front of us, right above eye level. There was a square of suet in a wire container hanging from a branch, likely placed there by a fellow birder. Suet is fat, and it's important for birds in the winter. Woodpeckers, blue jays, cardinals, sparrows, and many other species use suet as fuel to get them through a cold night. Whoever lived in that brownstone was a good egg.

In silence, we watched the downy hang from the wire container and poke its beak into the rich suet. It must have needed that sustenance because it stayed for a good minute, then flew up and away.

"That's a woodpecker," she said.

"Yes."

She shook her head, let out a small sigh, and smiled. "Well . . ."

"Yeah . . ."

We both heard the unspoken communication between strangers that our moment was complete and we would each be going our own way.

But before she turned to leave, she said, "Thank you. You know, I've never seen a woodpecker before." As she walked away toward Smith Street, I heard her say to herself, "A woodpecker in Brooklyn. What do you know!"

4

Bedouin

My job as an actor means I travel around the world to work, to go "on location." This particular month I'm on location in Albuquerque, New Mexico, shooting the movie *Maze Runner 2.* I arrive a few days before shooting begins, to get fitted for wardrobe, talk with the director, and meet the other actors.

I'm playing a scientist in a remote location, an apocalyptic landscape à la *Mad Max.* During my fitting, the costume designer and I both agree that my character doesn't have a large "closet," film jargon for all the different clothes the character will be wearing. The clothing she has for me to try on is exactly how I imagined it; we're on the same page, so we're done much earlier than scheduled. I leave wardrobe feeling energized and satisfied. I could go to hair and makeup, but again, in an apocalyptic landscape, hair products are not happening, and neither is much makeup.

The director is on set shooting, and I can visit if I'd like, but the set is far from downtown Albuquerque, where I'm staying. Production tells me tomorrow might be a better day to visit. I don't have any dialogue in the scenes I'm shooting this week, so no need to hole up in my hotel memorizing lines. Guess what that means?

I can see birds.

One of my ways into a new place is through the birds. They show me the lay of the land: Where am I? What's this landscape? Where's the water? The birds will know.

I look on Google Maps using both street and satellite views. Street view is clean and simple: I can see where there are lakes, rivers, streams, mountains, and green areas. Satellite view is helpful because it's not a representation but the true view from above, a bird's-eye view. I use Google Maps in conjunction with other apps, my go-to being BirdsEye, which is advertised as "a unique and powerful tool that helps you discover the birds around you and find the birds you want to see. See more birds with BirdsEye!" When I open the app and tap the "Nearby" button, up pops a list of all the birds that might be in the area based on real-time observations submitted to eBird, an online database of bird observations from all over the world. The app tells me what's around and, more importantly, what isn't, which is helpful because I often like to think I'm seeing the rarest bird in the world and the app will let me know, "Nope, sorry, that bird has never even been here!"

I use BirdsEye to scroll through the list of birds around Albuquerque and click on one I've never seen before, the curve-billed thrasher. A map opens, scattered with small red dots representing sightings of the curve-billed within the last thirty days. I tap on one of those dots and up comes Embudo Canyon—a hotspot, a location where one might see many different birds, and where someone had seen a curve-billed thrasher three days ago. If I go to Embudo Canyon I might see the curve-billed as well as fifty-three more species.

I drive to Embudo, one of several canyons along the Sandia Foothills. There's no parking lot, so I leave my car on a side street, grab my bins, and head into the canyon. As I walk along a gravel path, in the midday heat and silence, I remember a time I'd been in the desert years ago, I don't know where or why. But I remember now that I don't like the desert.

There's nothing living here: decrepit clumps of grass blotch the parched terrain alongside scraggly cactus bush things. The barren wall of the canyon looms in the distance, scorched by the sun. I like green. I like fecund, woods, water. I don't like this. And I am starting to disbelieve the BirdsEye app and the *Birding Hotspots of Central New Mexico* book that I brought in my suitcase. There's nothing here.

But I keep walking. Again, I don't know why, though perhaps, without knowing it, I'm practicing the principle I wrote about at the beginning of the book, "no contempt prior to investigation," coined by the philosopher Herbert Spencer, who goes on to say, "There is a principle which is a bar against all information, which is proof against all argument, and which cannot fail to keep a man in everlasting ignorance—that principle is contempt prior to investigation."

I've been working for thirty years trying to ingrain that idea into my psyche. As I mentioned, my default response to much of what life throws at me is *no,* so I've had to find ways to say *yes.*

Despite my frustration at the lack of life in Embudo Canyon, all the years of practicing to keep contempt at bay has paid off; I'm still here. But as I walk, that doesn't mean I don't feel contempt, just a little bit, for this landscape.

Then, a sound. A break in the silence. A kazoo underwater? I stop. Silence again. Not one thing is moving. I take a few steps, pretending to whatever made that sound that I didn't hear it. Don't mind me, I'm not aware of you. It starts again, the burbling kazoo. I scan the vista. Nothing.

But now, instead of pretending I don't hear it, I decide to creep toward the sound as covertly as I can, tiptoeing on the sandpaper gravel. Movement, rustle. And then I see the head of a bird, shaped like an Athenian helmet with a forward plume, bobbing over a small clump of brush. The bird warrior charges out, the helmet head atop a plump ball of a body, and darts into another clump of brush. A second one soldiers forth in the same getup and scuttles out from one clump and into the other. A third, fourth, fifth, all clucking that soft underwater kazoo sound.

Now their little helmets bob above a mess of hardy, hellish-looking flowers. The head on this bird is a stunning warrior mask, jet black from the tops of the eyes to the neck, encircled with a sharp white ring. The mask is fitted with a red-earth hood, a black curved crest dangling in front. The main body of the bird is slate gray with some buff in the front and that red-earth color, splashed on the wing. This is a little troop of Gambel's quail, one of two species of quail that call this canyon home, according to my app.

The Gambel's troop has gone quiet. But now that I know there is something living in here, my spirit lifts. My shoes scrape the dry rock sand as I turn to face another direction, and the scraping reverberates in the desert silence. As I finish my turn, I spot a hole in a cactus, with movement inside. I bring my binoculars to my eyes and meet the cadmium-orange eye of a curve-billed thrasher. Dull gray head, downward-curved bill long enough to hunt an insect on a cactus without brushing against the needles and blinding that beautiful electric-orange eye.

A second thrasher cuts through the air with a whit-whit, whit-whit, a sentinel atop a scraggly tree. Now I see the bird's full body, medium-size, like an American robin, nine inches in height. The thrasher in the cactus eyes the sentinel thrasher. Maybe they're a pair; maybe that's a nest inside the cactus. Birds don't chill out inside plants and trees unless there's a nest.

A lizard scurries across the ground at my feet. Then something flies past me—a cactus wren, two inches smaller than the thrasher but just as mighty, with a long, tough bill and a burnt sienna crown like that of the Gambel's quail but without the forward crest. It, too, has the warrior look, a slash of sienna extending from its rust-colored eye, white dashes against brown on the wing and brown dashes against white on the belly.

There's another bird, a group of birds, and another. It's four o'clock and the sun is less intense; of course, they lie low during high noon. After four is happy hour in the desert. I drink it up with them.

I've been here one hour and thirty minutes and traversed 0.05 miles. I've seen thirteen different species of birds, sixty-five individuals. If I'd turned around after the first few minutes, I'd have seen nothing.

Eventually, I walk off the desert land to paved streets lined with ranch-style homes and toward my rental car. I could have stayed longer; I don't have anywhere to go, and nobody is looking for me. But I'm filled to the brim with joy and can't take in any more. People think of nature as relaxing, and it is, but I'm an introvert, and the experience of the canyon feels as though I've been at a party with the birds for days. I need to recharge, to give my senses a reset. I need an ice-cold cappuccino.

There's a Bedouin saying that wherever you place your rug is home. Coffee shops are one of my Bedouin rugs. I'm a nomad of sorts, by virtue of my work—a fancier kind of nomad, but a nomad all the same, and I need a rug to ground me. There's always a Starbucks somewhere. I open up my Starbucks app.

I'm out of the canyon, but it stays with me, even as I arrive at a Starbucks on the outskirts of Albuquerque. Moments later, I'm sipping my iced cappuccino, and air-conditioning is soothing my senses. The sun is lower in the sky, and I imagine the way it looks out in the desert. The curve-billed thrasher's orange eye peers out from the cactus, watching the sun set.

In my mind, I'm on my Bedouin rug with the birds. I am home.

5

Cedar Waxwing

My first time seeing a cedar waxwing up close, it was not a living, breathing bird but a tattoo on a woman's ankle.

The young woman, her pant leg rolled up, shared how a cedar waxwing had saved her life. She had tears in her eyes as she told the story, and the audience mirrored those tears back as they listened. I was part of that audience, but I was there in another capacity as well. I was one of the judges at the third-annual tattoo contest at the Biggest Week in American Birding Festival. A few years prior, Kim Kaufman, the director of the festival, had had one of those *what if we . . . ?* moments and had created an event that incarnated one of Emily Dickinson's most famous lines: "'Hope' is the thing with feathers."

That was my first year judging. I thought it would be a good time, fun. By the end of the contest, my throat hurt from holding in tears; I didn't want to break down sobbing and steal the spotlight away from the courageous contestants.

To enter the contest, one must have a tattoo of a bird. There are three judges, who rate the tattoo on a scale from 1 to 5, using three criteria: story, design, and pain level. The first two criteria I understood, but I needed some tattooed folk to explain the pain-level criterion. Getting a tattoo involves some pain, but some areas of the body will hurt more than others. There is such a thing as a tattoo pain chart, ranking body parts by tattoo pain levels.

When a contestant's name is called, they emerge from the audience and make their way up to the area in front of the judges' table, where they show the judges and audience their tattoo and tell the story behind it. The winner of the contest receives a new pair of binoculars. That's a big-deal prize. For a birder on a budget (and many are) it's literally a new pair of glasses. After all the contestants have had their turn, the judges turn their chairs away from the audience and passionately yet quietly discuss who will take first, second, and third place.

There were eighteen contestants that year. I would love to share them all, but I'll focus on first, second, and third place. This is how I remember their stories.

THE FIRST CONTESTANT called was the perfect leadoff hitter: a big guy who strutted toward the judges' table, peeled off his shirt, spread his arms like wings, and revealed a huge great horned owl covering his whole back. He moved in a slow circle, his arms outstretched, showing off his owl tattoo like a peacock.

He loved great horned owls. He had seen one when he was a little boy and had never forgotten it. But honestly, he just wanted to go big with the tattoo. He wanted another bird tattoo but didn't have the room.

Pain level: 5 / Design: 5 / Story: 2

Even though he didn't win any prize, I felt compelled to give him an honorable mention for starting the contest off with gusto.

THIRD PLACE WENT to a young man radiating sweetness but with the look of a scruffy skateboarder. When he turned his back to the judges and lifted the back of his shirt up to his neck, there was a barn owl, wing tips touching each shoulder blade, talons tucked up and out ready to catch prey, eyes focused. Simply drawn with subtle color, design in service to the owl.

He hadn't liked birds when he was little. An owl trainer visited his school, and he watched the bird poop and almost threw up. He was headed toward studying marine biology, but then he read *Guardians of Ga'Hoole,* a fantasy book series, and everything changed. The main character is a barn owl, and the story saved him in a lot of ways. Now he volunteered at a raptor rehabilitation center.

Pain level: 4 / Design: 3 / Story: 4

SECOND PLACE WAS captured by a nice-looking man in his thirties, who confidently approached the front. He unbuttoned his shirt and pulled back one side, revealing a dignified vulture in black ink above his heart.

He remembered going through old nature books as a kid and coming across the bearded vulture or lammergeier, one of the rarest vultures in the world. It eats the bone marrow of huge animals, as big as giraffes, by dropping their bones against rocks. It has a fiery orange crown and neck from bathing in sulfur springs, and of course, a beard. His family had come to the United States undocumented from Spain, and he felt the need to reconnect to his roots. The lammergeier seemed to hold the key. Eventually, when he was cleared to travel, he went to the Republic of Georgia, where a vulture expert took him to a lammergeier nest. From that moment, he vowed to dedicate his life to raptor conservation. The tattoo was from a sketch he had drawn of one in the field.

Pain level: 3 / Design: 3 / Story: 4

NEXT, A YOUNG WOMAN stood in front of everyone and lifted her pant leg, revealing a tattoo of a cedar waxwing perched on a branch. It was an elegant and simple tattoo capturing the cedar waxwing's hard lines and bold contrasts. The woman's cheeks were red from being on stage in front of a large group of people and exposing not only her flesh but her story as well.

Her story went like this.

She had gone off to college and fallen into a deep depression. She didn't leave her bedroom. She grew suicidal. One day, she looked out her window and there was this bird. She'd never known a bird could be so beautiful. The bird came to her window the next day and the day after that. She started looking forward to it. And then one day it didn't come to her window, so she left her dorm room to look for it. She got outside. She started to notice other birds. And then she met people who liked birds. She joined a bird club at school, and now she was studying to be an ornithologist.

Pain level: 2 / *Design:* 2 / *Story:* 5

Her tattoo wasn't the best one. But she won.

She won because of the story. And her story impressed itself on me, like a memory tattoo, so that now, when I see a cedar waxwing, the memory runs up to meet it.

That happens with bird experiences; they fly in, nestle deep within my memory, and never leave. But they don't go dormant. They stay alive and active to new connections in the natural world, especially with their avian counterparts.

I WAS UPSTATE, at the kitchen sink washing the dinner dishes, when I registered an intermittent high-pitched sound. It had been tugging at me like a toddler does when they need to tell you something important, but you're so far in your grown-up world you don't even know they're there.

I turned off the water and listened for the sound, a sound that I had heard once before. I retraced my birding-memory steps and landed in Menil Park, Houston, Texas.

Sitting on the grass, in the middle of a patch of tranquil green in Houston, I had heard that same sound and followed it into the leaves of the sprawling live oak trees surrounding the park, where I met a stately bird with a crisp black mask.

It's a bird so perfect it doesn't seem real; it stands erect like a fine wood carving. Head feathers are slicked back, but instead of falling gently on the back of the head they veer up and out into a dignified mohawk. It sports a swashbuckling black eye mask. A sleek contour, composed of silken golden-brown feathers, merges into soft yellow, a dash of waxen red at the wingtips and a drop of bright yellow at the tip of the tail.

That day, as I'd watched the buzzing flock of Zorros flit from one live oak to the next before leaving the park, I'd learned that cedar waxwings travel in flocks. Not all birds do, but waxwings travel together, and they are known for eating fruit. They eat so much fruit, they can get intoxicated on overripe berries that have fermented.

Now, at home, just as I'd done in Houston, I followed the sound—or tried to. Rarely do I hear a bird sound and then, presto, locate it. It's usually a process, with stops and starts, highs and lows, but with persistence I usually find the bird. So many of life's discoveries happen when I stay that extra uncomfortable minute, past the point of restlessness and boredom.

The cedar waxwings' sound is tricky because it's really a call—a series of high-pitched call notes rushed together, sometimes too high for my ear to register. Or I mistake it for a mechanical sound. I zigzagged around the yard on a wild waxwing chase.

Finally, we met at the tree closest to the house, the one-hundred-year-old silver maple tree that stands in the front yard. There were about eight to ten waxwings. They stayed within the tree as opposed to flitting off to another, but they still had the restless energy, flying from branch to branch.

My attention kept returning to two specific waxwings. One of them held an insect in its beak, an inchworm. Oh good, they'd gotten food from the tree. And then: the waxwing stepped toward the second bird on the branch and offered the worm. The second bird took the worm with its beak and made this sequence of moves:

Turn head
Step to the right
Step back to center

Turn head toward the other
Offer worm

The first waxwing took back the worm, tossed its head to the side, and repeated the sequence. Hmmm, maybe it's an adult feeding a juvenile. That's probably what's going on, I thought. But then why isn't the other one eating the worm? No, it's something else.

By the fourth repetition of the sequence, I realized it was a dance with precisely choreographed steps.

I made an involuntary, guttural sound in my throat, a wordless uttering, a muffled gulp of gratitude and joy.

Those two cedar waxwings were engaged in something specific. Their actions revealed an agreement of sorts: I'm giving you this worm knowing that you will give it back. A worm is valuable—one would only risk losing food if there existed the possibility of something more valuable. A future?

The two waxwings acknowledged each other's potential before beginning the dance. And now the steps were solidifying that awareness into a bond. Among certain species of birds, the male will perform a specific dance for the female, a behavior called lekking, but this interaction was a collaboration as opposed to a one-man show, with choreography more akin to a trust fall. And the behavior is not unique; I'd learned that many bird species have complicated mating rituals—specific moves, repeated, not random, a dance to make life.

Suddenly, they all took flight, combining with another flock that I hadn't noticed in a nearby tree, and flew west, into the setting sun, about twenty-six in all now, maybe more. It's hard to count birds. They flew perhaps a quarter of a mile, and I followed them with my eyes, trying not to blink, to keep the connection alive between us. The group arced back, then split into two, settling again into the same two trees.

After only a few minutes, they all took off again. I watched them, holding fast to the invisible line connecting us, letting go when there was nothing but sky. And in that empty blue, I could imagine all the cedar waxwings I'd ever seen.

I made a vow to plant shrubs that produce berries, so I would have something to offer them when they came back—my human attempt at displaying behavior that says, "I like you."

6

Swifts

I heard what sounded like an electric current, around 7:00 p.m., above the parking lot of Snap Kitchen. I was in Austin, Texas, shooting a TV series in the fall of 2016, and I was just about to pick up a healthy prepared meal after a long day of work.

I looked up, expecting to see sparks flying from utility wires, but the wires were silent. Like a dumbfounded dog, I looked away and then back up again, thinking I had missed something. My gaze reached beyond the wires to the high sky, where I noticed a group of small, black birds, their flight pattern erratic but focused—skilled pilots with a daredevil streak. They suddenly zipped away before I could determine what exactly I was looking at. My feet took me to the car, against the wishes of my stomach, which wanted to get some dinner at Snap Kitchen.

I drove slowly around a residential neighborhood, stopping at every block so I could crane my neck out the window to get a wider view.

As I bobbed and weaved down the street, I ran through my mental bird encyclopedia: smaller than a pigeon, an unusual flight pattern, in a group rather than a lone individual—maybe something in the swallow family? Possibly, but the tail looked different; swallows have a forked tail. And I didn't remember swallows flying so high in the sky.

My mind screeched to a halt. I stopped the car and pulled out my iPhone, opening up a *real* bird encyclopedia, the Sibley app. David Sibley is the creator of one of the most respected and well-known series of bird guides. Not only does he know birds down to their DNA, but he can draw them. The Sibley app follows standard guidebook protocol with information about a bird's length and wingspan measurements, what it sounds like, where it nests. There are filters you can apply to help narrow your search.

I put in the state Texas, the month September, and directed the search results to show only common birds. You can further refine by all sorts of characteristics like primary color, secondary colors, habitat, size. But by entering just a place, time, and "common," I'd narrowed the possibilities down to forty species. I navigated to results in the swallow family and saw there was only one species of swallow here: the barn swallow. But I'd gotten to know the barn swallow, who often visited my house upstate, so I had an intuitive sense that these were not barn swallows. I clicked on an option to show similar species to the barn swallow and was presented with eleven birds. On sight, I was able to eliminate all but two: the chimney swift and the purple martin. I then consulted BirdsEye about what birds had been reported in the area. No purple martins. But yes, chimney swifts.

I resumed driving slowly through the neighborhood, hoping no one thought I was up to no good. And then I heard that sound I had heard in the parking lot, which Sibley describes as "single high, hard chips run together into rapid uneven, twittering, chattering series." I knew the swifts were close. I leaned over the steering wheel as far as was safely possible while looking up through the top of the windshield. Seeing a black flash, I pulled over and got out of the car. I found them chattering away, gathered in the sky. And then suddenly they were gone. Poof. Gone.

When I got home that night, I dived into swift world.

The chimney swift is a small black bird. Once it leaves the nest, it will spend most of its life airborne, touching down only to nest or roost. Swifts even drink and bathe on the wing. To drink, they fly low over the water and dip their bill in. To bathe, they glide down to water, executing a deft belly flop and springing back up, thereby spraying water through their feathers. When they do rest, they do it vertically, they do not perch; in fact, they cannot perch. Chimney swifts are too back-heavy and their feet are too weak for them to balance on branches, but they can hang upside down from the tiny ledges and cracks along a vertical surface. They've adapted to do so in the chimneys that give them their name, where they make their nests and roost in the fall before they migrate back south.

A swift's appearance is similar to that of a bat, despite one being a bird and the other a mammal. Their habits are also similar: at dusk, when swifts descend into their chimney, bats emerge in a living charcoal stream. In Austin, there's a bridge with an enormous bat colony underneath it, and, as the sun sets, thousands and thousands of bats ascend into the skies and eat millions of insects.

Like bats, swifts eat insects, whose populations are threatened by climate change and habitat destruction, so the swifts are also at risk. Swifts' numbers are declining so quickly that they're headed for "Vulnerable" on the International Union for Conservation of Nature Red List of Threatened Species; that's one step away from "Endangered" and four steps away from "Extinct."

Conservationists have organized efforts to save swifts. A valuable tool is collecting data. On four weekends in the fall, two weekends each in September and October, you can aid conservation efforts by counting the number of swifts entering a chimney. But how do you find these chimneys? Since 2011, the Chimney Swift Conservation Association has compiled a spreadsheet of active chimneys in North America. During my swift deep dive, I discovered that one such chimney was at an Austin elementary school mere blocks away from the house I was renting.

At dusk, I pulled up to a typical school scenario: chain-link fence, well-trodden grass, old cement basketball court, kind of quiet. I didn't see the chimney, and I didn't see any swifts. I walked around the perimeter and finally came upon the chimney—just a medium-size unremarkable old chimney, made out of brick. But that swift roost spreadsheet said this was a big-deal chimney. What were they talking about?

I stepped onto the small grass field. Being at school after hours was weird, too quiet—it felt as if it should be full of loud noise and play, not a place to be alone. I was tempted to turn around because the whole thing seemed like a bust, but I kept walking toward that chimney and then noticed a woman sitting in a lawn chair facing it. She was middle aged, and her clothes were practical: hiking pants and a Patagonia vest. She had a small notebook in her hand, binoculars hanging around her neck. I experienced that feeling of sunny relief when, after wandering lost in the woods, you find the well-worn trail with a friendly sign.

I asked her if this chimney was a roosting site. She nodded her head yes and told me she was a swift counter.

I sat on the grass beside her and looked up: nothing but blue. But I didn't lose heart, because I was sitting next to a swift counter. We didn't say much, which is typical with birders: the humans are second to the birds and we both knew it. I relaxed and looked around.

The place had sprung to life without me noticing. Dogs were running with their owners nearby; kids were riding bikes. It wasn't tumbleweeds after all.

The swift counter suddenly put her binoculars to her eyes. I looked where she was aiming but didn't see anything with just my eyes. I looked through my binoculars instead and saw what she saw: a small group of swifts doing the erratic flight I had seen the other night while driving. They were coming this way. I scanned the sky and saw swifts approaching from another direction. There were now twenty to thirty swifts flying above us, closer to the earth than their usual cloud-high flight, but still moving in that swooping, zooming pattern.

A few swifts dropped away from the scattered group and began flying in a circular motion, counterclockwise. Another swift joined, and another and another, forming a ring wide and loose enough for other birds to enter easily. The number of swifts flying in the circle increased, but their energy remained relaxed and easy; this pace continued for some minutes.

At 7:36 p.m. the sun dropped below the horizon, signifying the start of civil twilight. I didn't know at the time that there was such a thing as "civil twilight," but now I do, thanks to swifts, bats, owls, and nocturnal migration. Twilight is the time between night and day when there is still light out but the sun is below the horizon: morning twilight is dawn and evening is dusk. Astronomers define the three stages of twilight based on how far the sun is below the horizon: civil, nautical, and astronomical twilight.

When I saw the first swifts gather, the sun had just set, entering civil twilight, which lasts about twenty-five minutes, the approximate time it takes for the sun to move six degrees below the horizon. The gentle rays of refracted light illuminated the swifts' circular congregation. New swifts continued to fly in from all directions, some alone, some in small groups, and entered the circle without missing a wingbeat.

The energy of the ring changed with the setting sun: with each degree the sun dropped, the ring of swifts gathered momentum, spinning faster but never frenzied, with the school chimney at its center. I had no idea how many swifts ultimately were in the ring; the swift counter said it was well into the hundreds.

They spun round and round, and then suddenly one swift dropped into the chimney.

Who was that swift, the first one in? What was it like dropping into a dark void? How did they grab onto the wall? If they dropped in so fast, how would they not drop all the way down to the bottom? I'd be scared if I had to do that. Another swift dropped down, like an ember in reverse. Another and another slipped away; then all at once the swifts funneled into the chimney in one great inky swirl. The world had gone silent, no fighting or squabbling. Two or three swifts remained flying in the now-bare circle; they were the rear guard, a beacon for lost swifts. What swift was out there who didn't know where the chimney was? That would be nerve-racking, to have to get here by dark. Where would it sleep if it didn't make it?

A lone swift rushed in and tossed itself into the chimney. The rear guard kept flying, warding against the night. Another latecomer arrived and ducked down and in.

The countdown to near-dark began.

The rear guard made four more silent rounds, then descended.

The swift counter had tallied 1,024 swifts. After I got to forty-something, my brain shut down and didn't know what to do, so I just watched. She took out her small notebook and pen and wrote the date, the time, and, most importantly, the time of the last swift in. I was experiencing a feeling of ecstasy, but I don't think she was; she was a scientist and had seen this before, though I did see her smile as she folded up her lawn chair. We said goodbye—no plans, no exchange of numbers. I sat back down on the grass and stared at the chimney for about ten minutes, until it was so dark I couldn't really see it anymore. All twilights had passed.

The next day I went to a local hardware store and bought a foldable lawn chair. I finished work before sunset and raced to the swifts. The counter wasn't there. People were running their dogs on the school's playing field, and I felt weird putting my chair down facing a chimney. But I remembered past experiences of feeling weird when out birding, and what usually happened was what happened tonight. As I looked up at the circling swifts, a woman with her dog looked up too. "What are those?" she asked.

I said, "They're called chimney swifts."

"Oh really? I thought they were bats."

"Yeah, I know. They look like bats. But no, they are swifts. They're going to go into that chimney in about a half hour."

"Really?"

"Yeah."

She didn't stay to see the show, but that was fine. She left knowing that something was flying, something that was not a bat, something called a swift that had a life.

I am drawn to that life, and I'm not sure why. But I still feel that same urgency I felt in the Snap Kitchen parking lot when I hear their high-pitched twitter. Maybe because I know they're in trouble. One less here, one less there, and they move from Vulnerable to Endangered. Every swift counts.

In the spring and summer, often, I hear them when I'm standing on a corner in a town, a city, a suburb. You can find them any time of the day because they don't stop flying. But it's at sunset in summer, when the day is soft and the insects plentiful, that I look to join the end-of-day party: small groups diving through the sky, teaching their young how to catch insects.

I hear them in places that surprise me, like in Red Hook on Van Brunt Street, or above P.S. 29 in Carroll Gardens, Brooklyn, or on Sixth Avenue in New York City, or on Coffee Street in Houston. In the autumn, when I hear swifts, it is a call for adventure—one of those thrilling opportunities that birds offer, a Willy Wonka golden ticket.

I've gone in search of their roost in a few cities now; I hear them, and then I see them, usually six or seven, high up, catching their last meal of the day. As they zoom off to their mysterious destination, I zoom off in my vehicle, navigating obstacles like roads, laws, and restricted views.

I heard the high-pitched twitter of the swifts when I was

visiting my mom in Lombard, Illinois, forty miles west of Chicago. There were a few in the sky near her house. It was September.

My mom is always up for an adventure. Her curiosity, her noticing of the wild things living around us, helped awaken my receptors to the natural world.

Before sunset, we got in the car in search of their roost.

It helps to know where all the public schools are located because those have the biggest and oldest chimneys. Mom likes maps, directions, a sense of location, and landmarks. She knew all the elementary schools and told me to start with Hammerschmidt Elementary.

I didn't see a chimney in the front of the building, so I pulled around back to a small parking area where the teachers probably parked. Back there we found the chimney. I turned the car around so we could face it.

There were no swifts in sight. And there might not be. What's tricky about searching for roosts is this: swift arrival times can vary, and chimney preference can as well.

I've waited at a chimney, believing it was the winner, only to have no swifts appear. I've left chimneys that seemed like a dead-end date and raced to another that had promise but that also turned into a dead-end date. I've raced back to the first chimney, just in case, and gotten there as the last swift was taking its bow.

I got out of the car while my mom stayed in the passenger seat. No need for her to get out yet. I sat on the hood of the car, cupped my hands behind my ears to make a mini satellite dish, and closed my eyes. Ambient sound: two kids playing, a robin tut-tutting at something. The gambler in me was unsure. Should Mom and I just enjoy ourselves in the quiet? Sit in the newness of an area that wasn't in our everyday, the back of an elementary school at dusk? Or should we race to another school that might be a bust? I needed to also factor in that I couldn't drive as fast or crazy with Mom in the car.

Then I heard a swift. Mom did too. I yelled out, "Mom!" And she said, "I know!"

Five swifts flew a wide berth above us, disappearing and reappearing. They seemed to have other things on their mind, but it was encouraging. More swifts came in. As it got darker and more arrived, I knew we had a roost site.

The ring formed, maybe forty swifts.

I was on the hood and Mom was still in the car; that was her preferred watching place for now. That first swift took the leap and dropped in. Circling. Circling. A second swift dropped in. Moments later, a third. And then the funneling began. I counted roughly forty. I'm still not good at counting birds. I pulled out my iPhone and opened the eBird app. I entered the time, place, and number of swifts. I knew that data would help scientists but also some curious soul who wanted to find a roost. It was from someone else's eBird data that I had found this site.

After the last swift took the leap, Mom and I sat in the car for a moment in the dark. I imagined all the swifts hanging on the walls of the chimney. And then I realized, there were kids who went to that school because it was a school. I hadn't even thought of the children. An hour or two before they'd arrive at school in the morning, a funnel of swifts would emerge from the chimney. I'd never seen swifts leave a chimney. I'd never even thought of them leaving, only arriving.

My mom visited with me every night while I was there, but even after I left, she continued to visit the chimney through September and October. She often left me a short message about what she'd seen—her swift report.

In mid-October, she said there had been three nights in a row with no swifts. She was pretty sure they had departed for their southern climes, along with billions of other birds who migrate south in the fall.

The following fall, in September, I got a call from my mom one night around 8:00 p.m. She was distressed.

"Lili, a terrible thing has happened. I just went to the Hammerschmidt school to watch the swifts roost, and there were no swifts! There's some contraption up on the chimney now. Some steel bar or something, and I don't think they can get in. What are we doing to do?"

I furrowed my brow and tried to think. I felt nervous in my stomach. I had a bad feeling.

What if that chimney at the Hammerschmidt school was the last chimney in the area? Where would the swifts go at night? How would they survive? They'd worked all spring and summer rearing young, and now they were trying to fuel up and keep warm before their migration to somewhere in

South or Central America. I needed to know if this was a temporary thing or if it was permanent.

Mom was really distraught.

"Mom, I was planning on coming out that way. I don't think I can get there now, but I'll be there within a month or two, and we'll look into it."

Mom continued to visit the chimney that fall, but no swifts ever showed up.

It was a cold day in early December when my mom and I drove to the chimney at the Hammerschmidt school. We drove around the back, and I got out of the car to look. Yes, there was some metal band around the top of the chimney and some rods.

School was in session and the building was locked. I rang the buzzer and a nice woman from administration came to the door. I wasn't sure what I was going to say. It is always awkward when you're trying to get help for birds.

"Hi, my name is Lili Taylor and, this is sort of strange, but I'm a birder. I'm on the board of the National Audubon Society." As the words left my mouth I realized how silly this sounded, but I had no idea how to do this—and it did sort of sound official. I kept plunging ahead.

"And are you aware that there's a chimney in the back that a bird called the swift uses?"

"A swift?"

"Yes, do you know that bird, the swift?"

"Ah, yes, I think I do."

She craned her head up in the direction of the chimney

without much luck. She was standing in the doorway, using the door to block the wind—and maybe even to block the old lady and younger lady from entering the building.

"Is there someone I can talk to who might know? Like the janitor? Or something?"

"Yes, you can get in touch with Joe, the maintenance man. He's over at the Madison School a couple of blocks away."

"Wonderful, I'll do that. Thank you so much."

Mom and I walked into the Madison School and asked another nice lady if we could talk to Joe, the maintenance man. Joe was out doing things. He was a very busy man. He had to take care of a number of schools in the district.

I asked the woman at the desk if she knew about the chimney and the swifts. She also said she kind of knew swifts, but I wasn't convinced. She gave me Joe's email.

I tried to reach him a few times, but he was always out fixing something at another school. I allowed the issue to fade out of my mind. It was one of those tasks in life that requires some oomph, some stamina to keep taking those small, uncomfortable, and at times meaningless steps.

Maybe I wasn't sure what I would say to Joe if I did get him on the phone. Maybe I was secretly hoping he'd always be out. I've encountered this before, this complex, confusing gray area where people and wildlife try to coexist: outdoor cats, areas of beaches closed to nesting birds, loggers' jobs taken away because an owl needed those same trees.

I visited Mom over the summer, and we went to the school. The chimney was gone.

I knew chimneys were declining in the United States and with them the swift population, but witnessing it in real time transformed what had been an abstraction into a reality.

These days, if a large chimney isn't being torn down, it is most likely being capped shut. If you do a search on chimney swifts, pest control options will come up. A homeowner hears a foreign noise in their chimney and calls for help. The chimney sweeper comes and disposes of the birds and the nest. The homeowners never know what was in their chimney. The sweeper may know a little bit more because they see the so-called problem. But they don't *know* the chimney swift.

Hazardous old chimneys, capped chimneys, newer construction favoring metal flues over brick chimneys, conversion from coal and wood to electric and oil—there is little a person can do about all that. That's where laws, regulations, and institutions show their mettle.

But what can a person actually do? I went online in search of groups who were helping swifts. I found one in Wisconsin (right next to Illinois), the Wisconsin Chimney Swift Working Group. I went to their page titled "How Can I Help?" The first way to help is to let people know that swifts are here and that they can be helped by way of a few practical actions. One thing everyone can do is identify where chimney swifts are nesting and report those sightings to eBird.

Chimney owners should keep the top open and the damper closed from April through October to provide a nest site. And one can work with local conservation groups to help preserve existing chimney swift roosting and nesting sites. It's usually easier to restore what is there than to build from scratch. Though there are towers one can build for chimney swifts, called "faux chimneys," more studies need to be done on their efficacy, and the Wisconsin Chimney Swift Working Group suggests holding off on building towers for now.

While I look for specific ways I can help, I will continue to report every swift I see. I'll keep an eye out for roosting sites and decaying chimneys. And when someone sees me looking toward the sky, I'll get over my nerves and tell them I'm looking at a swift, it has a life and it's worth knowing. Then I'll ask them to stay and watch with me.

7

Tribute in Light

If you are in New York City on the night of September 11 and you look into the sky, you will see two massive beams of light rising into the sky. They are so tall and bright you can even see them from Brooklyn. Those beams of light have a name and purpose: the Tribute in Light, to honor the victims of 9/11. If you were able to get closer to those lights, you would see what look like dust particles swimming in the beams. Those *particles* are birds. And they are trapped within the two beams of light.

I volunteer with NYC Bird Alliance, formerly known as New York City Audubon, on the night of September 11 to help those birds get out of the light—an endeavor run by Dustin Partridge, the chief scientist at NYC Bird Alliance, and Andrew Farnsworth, an ornithologist at Cornell Lab of Ornithology. He is part of a team of scientists at Cornell that helped create a program, Birdcast, which uses weather radar and machine learning to forecast bird migration, providing real-time predictions of when they migrate, where they migrate, and how far they will be flying.

Birds, just like raindrops, are detected by a radar beam that tells us when to expect a downpour—or in this case, a migration. We're all familiar with the Doppler weather radar map that's filled with angry red, yellow, and green churning violently toward us while the weatherperson warns us trouble is coming.

But how different it feels to look at the BirdCast map, filled with electric blue, bright orange, and pink against a bold black. During the day the BirdCast map is pitch black, but come night, if the winds are favorable to the birds' flight, little blue dots appear on the black map, and then all at once, the dots bloom into blossoms of electric blue, melding into one. That explosion of blue is hundreds of thousands of birds taking off at the same time in different locations, usually right after sunset.

The majority of birds migrate twice a year: in the spring they fly north to breed, and in the fall they fly south, mostly to the Southern Hemisphere, where they spend the majority of their lives, a reality we are only beginning to understand. Over the past ten years, novel analytical models, data products, and technical advancements in the ability to track birds using tiny geolocators have provided bird's-eye views into their migratory routes and stopover locations.

The fall migration includes all the youngsters born that spring, literally flying into the unknown. I'm thinking of a juvenile male rose-breasted grosbeak, whom I saw grow up one summer in upstate New York. I don't know the actual night in

September he left to go south; I just know that one day I didn't see him anymore. What night did he leave? And how did he know to pick that night? How did he know the wind was right? Like airplanes, birds need tailwinds, that is, the wind behind them, as opposed to headwinds, when the wind is coming straight at them. Could he sense his parents were going to take off? What if he didn't sense it and saw his parents fly away one day but thought they were just going somewhere in the neighborhood?

Regardless, he's on his own now. His DNA knows he's going somewhere in South America, but it doesn't know how to avoid the two light beams 120 miles south as the grosbeak flies. There is a high probability that the young bird will pass over New York City because it lies under the Atlantic Flyway, one of the four American flyways that birds use, like we use interstate highways. The young bird will also likely fly over New York City because birds are drawn to city lights, for reasons scientists still don't completely understand.

One theory is that the bright lights block the lines in the north-south magnetic field that birds use to navigate and block out celestial signposts guiding their way. This can mean that birds either crash into a lighted building or circle within a cage of light until they drop dead from exhaustion.

Artificial city lights kill three hundred million to one billion birds a year and are a leading cause of the staggering decline in bird populations. So scientists are furiously collecting data on the ways artificial light affects nocturnal migration, using geolocation devices and the same radars that are used to track storms. But the only way scientists can monitor the health of the world's ten thousand bird species is by engaging the public, everyday citizens who care about birds and the places they need.

Because of people who care about birds, BirdCast can now forecast the exact number of birds flying over your county and at what time. Some of the data collected during migration has even contributed to programs like Lights Out, a national effort by a network of cities to provide safe passage for migrating birds by working with building owners and managers to turn off excess lighting.

Scientists are also working to determine what buildings are causing the most bird fatalities. They know this because there are dedicated volunteers who walk the streets early in the morning after a night of migration and collect injured and dead birds from the sidewalks. For injured birds, if the city has a wildlife rehabilitation center, they will be transported there. In the case of New York City, they are taken to the exceptional wildlife hospital, Wild Bird Fund, founded by Rita McMahon. For each deceased bird, its location is entered in a database called D-bird, and over time it becomes obvious what buildings are responsible for most bird fatalities by the sheer number of dead birds on its doorstep. Each major city has at least three or four bird-killing buildings. If they simply turned out the lights at night for roughly two weeks in the spring and fall, millions of birds' lives could be spared.

The first time I helped turn out the lights for birds was on September 11, 2017, and it was only for twenty minutes, not two weeks.

I arrive at 7:45 p.m. to the address that was emailed to me, a parking garage. I step into the garage and find no sign of anything having to do with the Tribute in Light.

I back out and walk around the block, scanning for a friendly entrance, but end up back inside that garage because that's what matches the address I had been given. There's no attendant, nobody. I call out. An older black guy in navy blue shirt and pants comes out. "Hey, do you know where I'm supposed to go where all those birders are? Like on the roof or something?"

He says, "Birders?"

"Yeah, it's Audubon, connected to the Tribute in Light."

"Oh yes, yes, you go on through that door there, take the first elevator one floor up and then there's a second elevator and someone will be there—should be there—to take you to the place. Hey, wait a minute. I know . . . I know . . ."

"Yes, it's movie and TV."

"I knew it! I love your stuff. You are good."

"Thank you, my friend."

I follow his directions and make it to the rooftop. A big bouncer-looking guy is there, but he has no idea what I'm talking about when I tell him I'm there to monitor birds. I peer over his burly frame, scanning the roof for the Audubon folk. Even though there are massive beams of light, the roof is surprisingly dark. But I can eventually make out small groups occupying different areas of the roof.

I point to a group that looks focused and say, "I think those are my people there."

The big guy shifts his head a millimeter in the direction I'm pointing and turns back unfazed. "I don't know who they are."

I ask nicely, "Would you please let me go and get one of them so they can explain? Please."

He sighs, continues looking straight ahead, and moves to the side to let me pass. On my way toward the group, I have to move some heavy guardrails. This is already an adventure, and I haven't even seen any birds yet. As I approach the group, I see the Patagonia and North Face jackets, binoculars around the neck, baseball hats, and a woman holding a clipboard.

I go up to her. "Whew. I made it. I'm here to volunteer."

"Great. Let me get you started." She calls to a guy and says, "Are you on the North or South Tower?"

"North," he says.

"Okay, I'm going to have . . ." She turns to me. "What's your name?"

"Lili. Lili Taylor."

She moves closer to my face, inspecting me.

"Hey! I didn't recognize you in the dark. I'm so glad you could make it! I'm Susan, scientist for Audubon. I'm going to have you go to the North Tower with Doug. Doug! Can you give Lili the lay of the land?"

Doug says sure and Susan hands me a sheet of paper, filled

with an Excel-like grid, and a pencil with which I will fill in the time and number of birds seen on the half hour.

I head toward what they're calling the "North Tower," which consists of a large square platform about four feet high with forty-four spotlights. It's a giant horizontal Lite Brite. The lights are only interested in the sky, leaving the area surrounding the tower dark. About twenty-five feet from the light tower, I make out Doug casting a yoga mat on the asphalt garage roof.

Doug says, "I think I know you from the Prospect Park Bird Club. You're friends with Tom Stephenson, right?"

"Yes, I am. Hi."

"Hi."

Doug lays down on the mat, his feet pointed toward the tower, and brings his bins up to his eyes. I put down my backpack next to Doug, fish out an old towel, and copy his process, like a preschooler performing an important task for the first time. Just as I'm bringing my bins to my eyes, Doug says, "Did you mark the start time?"

"No, I didn't."

"Mark the start and end time. We count on the half hour."

"What exactly am I counting?"

"Birds. The number of birds that keep circling. When that number reaches a thousand, we tell Susan, and Susan will ask the light people to shut off the lights for twenty minutes."

"Gotcha."

I sit up and mark down "10:05 p.m., North Tower" on the

Excel sheet. I lie back down and bring the bins back to my eyes. I don't see anything really, and the little specks I do see really do look like dust.

I keep looking up at a rectangular beam of light that stretches up and beyond what I can see with my naked eye, or the bins for that matter. The light seems infinite. To the right of me, on the other side of the garage roof, is the south beam of light. There are ten volunteers per two-hour shift, grouped in twos, situated at specific locations on the roof. I don't know who or where the others are. There isn't much talking; we all go straight to work. I settle into a world of night sky and light beams.

I see a big dust-like being flutter across my field of vision. But it seems too focused for a speck of dust. It enters again from the direction it exited. It has a hint of yellow. It's a bird. Suddenly, I see more things in those beams of light. Lots of things. I see small pieces of what looks like confetti with a fan blowing on them. But instead of floating down to the ground they're zooming around like protons and neutrons. There are things pinging around up there.

"What are all those specks?"

Doug tells me, "We're mostly seeing insects right now. There are birds in there, but the majority of what we're seeing are insects."

Some of these insects are big, like a small bird. I didn't know they could look like that. Then a bird enters the frame. I'm beginning to distinguish between a bird and an insect and dust. The bird seems focused, the insect dizzied.

The view, little things moving in light, looks the same even if I move my binoculars up or down within the light. Usually, when you use binoculars, you are following a bird as it moves through its world. Birds don't stay still for long, so neither do you when you look at them. It was strange to stay looking at one thing without any information from the periphery.

There is no other view or reality to compare or contrast with the infinite light edged by black, filled with what look like energetic, infinitesimal life forms. This myopic view is one view, the only view, my only reality. I'm sitting on the lip of a huge petri dish, and this is where I'd always been.

A voice breaks in. "What time is it?"

"Time?"

"Yes, time," says Doug.

Oh, yes. I take the bins down and return to the roof of a garage on an autumn evening on September 11. The time is 10:29 p.m.

Doug says he saw seventeen birds. Oh. I'd seen two. Yikes. How the hell did he see seventeen? I was looking at the same thing he was. Were my two birds included in that seventeen? I highly doubt I saw something Master Birder Doug hadn't. We decide to mark it down as seventeen.

I record my first data entry ever: 10:30 p.m. Forty-nine degrees. Seventeen birds. Doug doesn't even remove his binoculars while I write this down. Hardcore. Second shift begins. I'm on until 2:00 a.m. I would like to take a break. Maybe someone has a table set up with hot water or coffee, snacks? I like breaks. But Doug doesn't even seem to have the word *break* in his vocabulary.

I find out Doug is a guide for a prestigious bird tour company. He takes birders on trips to the Arctic, Africa, India, New Mexico—a dozen trips a year. Doug and I can relate since we both live a mobile lifestyle that takes us away for long periods. It's nice connecting with someone else who lives this way. It's hard to understand if you aren't in it, just as working nine to five, five days a week, is difficult for me to comprehend.

It's midnight. We are allowed to take a short break as long as one of us stays on patrol. Guess who's taking the break at midnight? I wander over to a folding table and am thrilled to discover snacks; I grab a banana and a granola bar. I stroll to the brick wall at the roof's edge. With the beams of light behind me, I see dark sky. It looks like nothing is there, but I know for a fact there is a lot there. Andrew Farnsworth told us the north wind picked up, and he estimated there were thousands overhead.

I look north and see the Empire State Building. I've experienced bird migration from the rooftop of that building, so my imagination is full tilt as I picture the sky above it filled with a stream of birds. I look south and try to see the Statue of Liberty but can't get her in my vision. I turn around and lean back against the wall with an eye-level view of the two platforms.

There are dozens of insects swarming around the 7,000-watt lights, flying too close and bursting into flames upon impact, snuffed out of existence.

A security guard walks the perimeter of the platform with a hand broom, sweeping away the scorched gossamer debris. Fires are common: the lights are so hot a mere singed wing is combustible.

A monarch butterfly wafts toward the lights. A volunteer tries to redirect the butterfly, waving his arm to create a current that will blow the butterfly away. I feel like I'm watching a horror movie. The chief scientist waves her clipboard in the direction of the monarch, and that small force, combined with that of the arm-waving guy, puffs the butterfly away. A general sigh of relief releases from the small crowd.

I lie back down next to Doug. He allowed himself a break from the counting to watch the monarch escape tragedy. I bring the bins to my eyes and enter back into the world of beams, specks, and dark. There are a lot more birds now. A lot.

"Oh wow," I say to Doug.

"Yeah, it picked up."

"How many are you seeing?"

"I'm at about 759."

Again, I'm seeing what looks like fifty. I get very serious inside and summon my concentration, all my senses. I try not to think. Just look. Just *look*. My vision climbs slowly up the beam, pushing through the light. Some invisible birds become visible. I try counting but can't. But I am seeing more birds. It's as if I'm willing my eyes to go beyond what they can do. I remember they are a muscle and keep pushing. And I see more birds, with a kind of X-ray vision. I don't understand what I'm raying through, but it is happening.

There are so many birds, spanning all floors of the beam. More and more birds are dropping lower, a sign that their efforts at getting out of the light are failing. Doug thinks we are getting close to that special number, but close is not enough. It has to be one thousand—or literally a bird in hand.

Doug jumps up to consult with Susan, but there is no need, for in her palm lies a magnolia warbler, a male with bold streaks of black running down its yellow chest. I'm moved by how small it is—much smaller than the magnolias I'd watched flitting from tree to tree.

She will bring the bird in hand to the light people. But it is by no means a sealed deal that the lights will turn off. Each time it is a negotiation, a gentle explaining. It is a miracle we are even on this roof. The relationship between the Tribute in Light people and the folks at NYC Bird Alliance and Cornell Lab of Ornithology has been twenty years in the making. Andrew Farnsworth, the ornithologist from Cornell, said it took seven years for them to even start talking. They stayed with it, despite the slow progress, adjusting expectations and strategies for a long game, always with respect and courteousness, the skills of listening and empathy.

We all stand fixated on the beams of light as we await Susan's return with the verdict. There is no need to count anymore because the numbers had reached critical mass.

There is nowhere for the birds to go but down, their precious fuel burning out in the cages of light. They descend slowly, inexorably, gravity taking its toll. Their flight disordered, feeble. With each descent, their panicked flight calls increase, faint but piercing. Each call summons our instinct to help, to do something, but that instinct also has nowhere to go, so it paces and frets.

And then an explosion of dark. The beams are gone like a monster vanquished.

Susan the scientist emerges from the darkness met with a soft chorus of cheers. The lights will stay off for twenty minutes, the determined length of time it will take the birds to orient themselves and continue their migration.

We mill about for another fifteen minutes, jobless until the lights come on.

Once they do, we turn our attention to Andrew Farnsworth, binoculars up, standing alone closer to the beams, a captain at the bow of a ship, and wait for his all clear.

All the birds made it out. They are on their way.

It is now 1:20 a.m. I have forty minutes to go before I am relieved. No one is in a hurry to get back to their mats because there are no birds yet, so we meander back to our respective places, and when Susan calls out, "It's 1:30," we are all lying down and looking up. The beams fill up quickly with birds. This is a high-migration night. I still try to count, but I'm out of my league, really. I wonder if I should even be here. Am I taking the seat of a real ornithologist or a highly skilled amateur? I was upfront with Susan when I volunteered that I'm by no means an expert birder. But I think my skill set has its own usefulness: getting the word out, speaking on behalf of birds.

It's nearing 2:00 a.m. My shift relief is here.

Doug says, "Nice seeing you."

"You too, Doug. Take care."

I roll up my mat, leave the tally sheet with Doug, and say my goodbyes quietly.

I don't see the nice garage guy when I leave. I exit and walk as if I know where I'm going, but I don't. I know the area, of course: I've lived in the city for over thirty years. But I feel like I've come from another world—because I have.

I've been in the world of light and dark, birds, hope, and suffering.

I keep walking until I find a cab; there's no way I'm going underground for the subway.

In the cab, crossing over the Brooklyn Bridge, as I look behind me at the beams of light, I see the birds and then dust particles and then just the two beams. I think of the good people on the roof, helping another living thing keep living.

I exit the cab on the corner of my street in Brooklyn. No one is out. I have the borough to myself, but I don't feel alone. There is a marathon of birds above me.

8

Finches

I'm going to be shooting a TV show in New Mexico. I've filmed there a lot over the past fifteen years, based mostly in Albuquerque, but this time I'll be based in Santa Fe, and I'm resistant.

Part of the resistance is superficial, based on flimsy judgments: I have memories of being stuck in traffic in that little town center, and it seemed as if anywhere I went women were talking about turquoise jewelry. The place has a Hamptons vibe dressed in desert mountain style.

But the majority of my resistance stems from a deeper place: fear dressed up in judgment. We all have "new job jitters." Ninety percent of workers, when asked about beginning a new job, admitted to feeling nervous. And over half said it was scarier than skydiving.

My new job will also be in a new place. I'll be away, from February 1 through August 1, on "location," film parlance for shoots that take place out of the main towns of Los Angeles and New York City. I feel like a kid going off to camp and like a nomad. But the caravans we use today are fancy and expensive and we don't sleep in them at night. And at the end of the working day, everyone—crew and actors—leaves the area where we've been filming to return to their respective homes.

Except it's not really my home, but I must pretend that it is—just as I spend the day pretending I'm someone I'm not when the cameras are rolling. After work, when I open the door to my adobe rental, the existential fear greets me.

Who is the *I* in this new home? The externals that I have in my normal life that ground me in who I am—husband, child, friends, neighbors, dog, apartment—are not in this location. I'm dislocated, out of place. It goes with the job. I'm inhabiting a character, and the new location inhabits us, so it's not out of order per se, but it's uncomfortable.

The discomfort makes it harder to hear what's truly going on inside of me. I can't tell if my new rental house is wrong and must be changed immediately, if I really have a handle on the character, or if I'm way off base. I act on these feelings as if they were facts by asking the realtor if I can change houses and by taking aside Josh Brolin, my fellow actor who is playing my husband in the show, and asking if I'm about to be fired.

One day, early in the acclimation process, I was making my daily trip to Target to purchase some object, it might have been a throw rug or outdoor string lights that would make the house feel more like a home. I was stopped at a long traffic light, so long that I was not able to speed away from the inner whispers trying to get my attention. I felt like I was alone, on the top of a mountain, the cold whirring wind blocking me from my other selves.

And then I heard a song—the song of a finch. The stoplight turned green and I moved on, but the song did, too, carrying me three hundred feet before cross-fading into the song of a second finch, which then carried me three hundred feet more. Expecting to be dropped, I was delighted when I was passed gently to finch number three. And then there was the song of a fourth and a fifth—a serenade of finches on Paseo de Peralta. The finch parade warmed me on the top of that cold mountain. The wind died down, and I could hear myself a little better.

The house finch looks very similar to the house sparrow, that ubiquitous small, brownish bird, except the male finch has splashes of crimson red on top of his head and chest and the female has brown stripes on her chest. You can find them all over the United States, but for some reason I'm more aware of them in New Mexico—especially their song.

I realized I didn't know where they came from, so I checked. Sure enough, they originate from the Southwest. I never thought of them as a desert bird—they always seemed suburban to me—but that's maybe why they seem so at home here. They can actually be at home almost anywhere in the United States; they are considered one of the most adaptable birds, occupying one of the largest ecological ranges of any living bird.

In the metropolitan area of Santa Fe there was a lot of finch activity. I noticed the array of finches when searching the town for another thing, along with birds, that helps me locate myself:

a café. I love coffee and I love cafés, but during the pandemic I'd realized how important cafés were to me. I'd missed them so much that I'd gone to a favorite website of mine, mynoise.net, a "world of immersive and customizable soundscapes," to see if I could find the sounds of a café.

When you click on the sound, it brings up a new page with a thorough description and an equalizer-looking graphic with ten sliders, each slider representing an individual sound making up the total soundscape. This is where the website author allows users to customize the sound experience to one's own liking. For "café," here are some of the presets that I could play around with: restaurant, chatter, babble, cocktail party, cafe, table, kitchen. I'd brought down the *kitchen* noise, like plates and silverware, because I didn't want to be in a restaurant and brought up the *chatter* and *babble* sounds. I didn't leave my pretend café until the pandemic was over.

But now I'm out in the real world, searching for a cafe that I could anchor into. After visiting a half dozen, I settled on a café called 35 Degrees North: excellent coffee, friendly baristas, sturdy tables. Plus, it was a few blocks away from the busy town center and located on the second floor, so easily missed by tourists.

OVER TIME, I noticed patterns with the male finches on my walk from the car to the café and back again. They seemed to be singing from specific places. One sang on the balcony of a building next to the café; another sang on the corner of a hotel roof, a block away. I tried to chart the males' primary singing stations, in the hopes of creating a finch map in my mind, but it wasn't as easy as I thought.

Since that fateful day of the finch parade, it seemed like everywhere I went I was greeted by finches. I especially noticed their song when parking my car and moving from the dull interior into a vibrant exterior world: the grocery store near my house, Planet Fitness, and Garson Studios, where most filming took place.

The studio sits on the defunct campus of what was the Santa Fe University of Art and Design. The campus is about the size of a football field, smack in the middle of town. The school closed in 2018 due to bankruptcy, and the studio took up residency in 2020.

When you enter the main complex, the first thing you see is a dilapidated guard shack, a ripped sign taped to the window with the handwritten words "Student ID," an old office chair turned upside down. The flora and fauna that cover the campus are overgrown and disordered but not confused. The place is undergoing the natural process of ecological succession, namely, determining what natural community will succeed the next one over time.

Some of the dorms sit abandoned, but others are being used for addicts in recovery, and I heard one is being used as a shelter, but no one seems sure. On the way to the studio, along an inner road, Alumni Drive, about a two-block distance from the main entrance, as you drive past the derelict dorms, you often see some down-on-their-luck men hanging about, who, like the flora and fauna, are also in the process of finding their way.

Garson Studios is in no better shape than the rest of the place. Even though it's a fully functioning studio, it still houses the remnants of a college campus with a couple of big stages plopped onto it.

The place was put together fast, no time for sanding around the edges, following the motto "Use what's at hand and get to work." Film productions are remarkably agile, structured much like a military operation. Here the trailers are all gathered in one place, called Basecamp, a sort of mobile command center for the more fixed general headquarters of the production office. In this production, the trailers for the main cast are called two-bangers: two actors in separate units in one trailer. The exception is Josh Brolin; he had his own enormous, Elvis-like trailer, and I loved giving him shit for it. He didn't want that fancy trailer; his agents asked for it. The cast and crew love Josh. He's also the executive producer of the production, but you'd never know it. He's a worker among workers; generous and kind.

ONE DAY IN APRIL, I finished shooting early. I wasn't in my usual rush to get out of there after working a fifteen-hour day. Instead of walking quickly to my trailer to get undressed, I sauntered, and that's when I noticed two house finches flying in and out of this black metal thing attached to Josh's trailer, a device I later learned is called a transport hitch.

It was a pair, a female and a male. The male house finch has cadmium-red feathers on its head and upper chest with gentle streaks of brown on the belly. Cadmium has orange undertones, giving the red a glow brightness. The female has a base of beige-gray feathers with the streaks of dark brown covering its chest and belly.

This is what I observed: the male perched atop my trailer, situated right next to Josh's, and was eyeing the hitch, so I did too. The female flew out of the hitch and then flew away. She returned with blades of dried grass in her beak and alighted on top of my trailer for a moment, then flew into the hitch. I waited for her to exit again before barging into her space to investigate where she was flying into.

I ducked to get a look under the thing and discovered a rectangular opening, four by three inches. I reached my arm in, then down about three inches, and my hand touched grass.

I grasped the grass but was stopped mid-lift by the sound of the finches' panicked alarm calls to one another and to me.

Sometimes, when I get worried, I talk out loud. Feeling helpless, my inside thoughts force their way out in the hope they can help.

It's just me and the finches now, so I say, "No guys. No. You can't build a nest here." I continue to talk as I resume the destruction of their new home, removing the grass. "This trailer doesn't live here. It moves when we move to a new location." As I place the grass on the steps of my trailer, one of the finches flies into the transport hitch. "No, finch. No." It flies back out and then away, the second finch following.

They may be gone, but I know they haven't left. It is only a matter of time before she returns with blades of grass in her beak and flies into the hitch. The male is close behind and alights on my trailer to oversee. It does no good to pull out the grass; they will just keep rebuilding. I watch two more rounds of construction, imagining the trailer pulling away one day with baby finches tucked inside, the parents off finding food, returning with the seed of a coneflower, to emptiness.

Would it be the end of the world if that scenario played out? There are finches all around, building nests and procreating. Their population is healthy; they are listed as "Not Threatened," according to the International Union for Conservation of Nature Red List of Threatened Species, an inventory of the health of the world's biodiversity, classifying species at risk using nine categories: Not Evaluated, Data Deficient, Least Concern, Near Threatened, Vulnerable, Endangered, Critically Endangered, Extinct in the Wild, and Extinct. But I will continue to think about those finches, knowing I could have done something, some small thing, to meet them halfway. They are trying to survive with what is left, a transport hitch in place of a tree. Trees don't move like transport hitches do.

How can I help? A reparation for habitat destroyed?

I decide I'll pick them up a nest box at the hardware store. But meanwhile, I need to find Buddy, the teamster who oversees Josh's trailer. Buddy takes pride in taking care of Josh's trailer: he drives it, cleans it, fixes it. All of that is part of his job, but he goes the extra mile in stewardship and kindness. He loves grilling and once or twice a month makes a feast for the crew. He hopes to retire someday and open a restaurant.

Even though Buddy is sweet as hell, I still feel self-conscious and weird as I explain to him what's going on, wishing I was asking for something more normal, like how to turn the air conditioner on in the trailer. But Buddy wants to help. He's in. We look at the hitch, and he says he'll figure out some way to keep them from getting in. I'm so happy to have someone helping. I told him I'd be back soon, I'm going to the hardware store.

I love hardware stores; my family had one, E. B. Taylor Hardware, founded by my grandfather and taken over by my father—though he wasn't a hardware man, he was a writer. I visited our store a lot and worked there for stints during the summers. Because they feel safe and familiar, I can wander the aisles, allowing my imagination to travel, and I needed that freedom of mind in the Santa Fe Ace Hardware to hatch a plan for the finches.

Finding the actual birdhouse was the easy part. Most hardware stores sell at least one kind of birdhouse, though this Ace had a particularly nice one, designed for actual birds and not some cutesy, impractical arts-and-crafts piece designed for humans.

The challenge is where to put the birdhouse and how to mount it, in a spot safe from predators like raccoons, snakes, crows, ravens, foxes, cats, and rats. The best way to do that is to mount it on a pole, which is difficult to climb and away from places of easy access, like a tree limb. Yet I want it close enough to a tree that the finches have a place for quick escape if needed; we all need somewhere to flee to. But the pole is too complicated to implement.

As I walk up and down the aisles searching for a solution, my thoughts become more constricted, like when you work too long on the same math problem and the cost outweighs the benefits. I dig in and switch gears, shifting my narrow focus to a soft gaze, viewing the objects on the shelves as if I didn't know what they were for.

I come across a green five-foot steel post, the kind you see road signs mounted on, and I realize I can use it as a nest box post instead. The predrilled holes, running the length of the post, give me plenty of options to change the height of the box if needed.

I'm excited to find a solution, but then I realized the nest box doesn't have any holes in the back. Keeping my gaze soft and adopting a newcomer mindset, I see a pack of shims—those thin pieces of wood that you use to level things, like a folded napkin under a wobbly table. One on its own is too weak, but I can double them up, secure them to the post with zip ties, and then screw the nest box onto the shims.

I also grab a five-gallon bucket because why not, and three packs of zip ties in different lengths, an X-ACTO knife, bungee cord, duct tape, rope, and a small miraculous hammer with fifteen uses: unscrew the cap on the handle and various screwdrivers and other tools spill out.

Heading to the register, I make a U-turn without thinking.

It doesn't feel right leaving with only the nest box for the birds to reside in. A pang of empathy brings me back to when I was maybe ten or eleven, whatever the age is when we decide we are too old for stuffed animals. That day had come, so I rounded them all up, fondly bid them farewell, and put them in a carton destined for the attic. That evening, all alone in bed, one of those scary thunderstorms came down from the heavens and surrounded my house. I thought of my animals, abandoned in a cold, hard box, alone for the first time. No longer able to withstand the feeling of imagining how it felt to be them, I ran to get them, took each one out of the box, and gently placed them on the side of my bed against the wall.

I PROMISE I GENERALLY try not to anthropomorphize living things but instead try to take them in as they are. You could very well substitute *taking in* with the words *perceive, observe,* and *pay attention,* to name just a few. And the more I do that, the more connections light up some fundamental truths about human beings. Those truths remind me why I'm here and what my purpose is, something that I need reminding of quite often.

I've been aware of this concept, *taking in,* since I was a teenager; it was just dressed up differently by the acting pedagogy under which I trained. I learned it as "Be in the moment." Some acting teachers added some hambone to the mix by elongating the *e* for a full two seconds. I earnestly tried to use the phrase while I was acting, but I was never clear on how exactly to do it because it's not very *actable*—there's no specific action to ground me. I would try to be in the moment but always felt like I was failing, as there was no way to measure whether I was really there or not: What is the state of being? How do you *be*?

About twenty years ago, I started replacing "being" with "listening," and it's worked much better for me. There are specific, concrete ways to listen. The most important thing is that it involves the other actor rather than the lonely and existential act of being.

All this is to say, I try to be open to living things, but it's a work in progress. And that day, in that hardware store in Santa Fe, I needed to right my course after getting too sentimental imagining the finches would be sad if I left with just an empty nest box. I thought more clearly about what they need to survive: shelter, water, and food. So I grabbed a bird feeder, twenty pounds of black oil sunflower seed, and a fourteen-inch plastic planter tray to serve as a birdbath. I also grabbed a hummingbird feeder. Because why not?

RETURNING TO BASECAMP with my supplies, I smiled when I saw an enormous garbage bag covering the trailer hitch with rope wrapped snugly around, like you would cover a tree for winter. I loved that Buddy, and his teamsters, care enough to go to that extra length. I want to tell him how much it means to me, but it will have to wait because he's off doing something important.

I get to work setting up the finch habitat behind the trailers, an area the size of half a tennis court, full of dusty gravel and tumbleweed trash, edged off with the same chain-link fence that surrounds all of Garson Studios. There is one pine tree next to the fence, and that is the area I focused on.

The zip ties turn out to be the hero tool of the hour. I use over thirty zip ties between the nest box, feeders, and mounts. I don't like the look of the tips of the zip ties jutting out everywhere, so I cut them all down to the nub for a cleaner aesthetic.

The five-gallon bucket proves handy in carrying water from the production office to the birdbath. I didn't realize there was no source of water out here behind the trailers.

The last step is placing the grass I stole from the finches' first nest on top of the nest box, to indicate to them that this foreign object and the grass go together. I find an old folding chair and set up a perch twenty feet away, but the eyesores of strewn trash keep pulling my focus.

I remember that I have leather gloves belonging to my character in my trailer. I put them on, grab a trash bag, and think of the Swedes who jog and pick up trash, a practice called plogging, while I go about my chore. There is an intimacy to looking at the individual pieces of trash up close in an area that I pass every day. I still don't like it, but I'm slightly less disgusted now that the objects were made more real: a faded Mountain Dew can—who drank that? Flattened cardboard, a fossilized sock, a tattered box of Popeyes with some chicken bones bitten into, most probably by a critter. I wonder what critter. Who lives around here anyway?

By the end of the first day, fourteen house finches are gathered on or near the tube feeder filled with black oil sunflower seed. The chain-link fence has become a suitable perch for birds waiting in line for a spot on the feeder. House sparrows show up as well but are outnumbered by the finches. The plant tray—aka birdbath—is frequented often for both drinking and washing. No finch had entered the box by day's end, but everything else is a hit.

THE NEXT DAY, I wasn't scheduled to work, so there was no reason to go to the studio. But by late afternoon I was itching to see if any finches accepted my bid on the house, so I headed over.

The grass is still on top of the nest box. I open up the side of the box in the hope there is a blade of grass or two in there, but there is none. The feeder and water station are packed with finches and a few sparrows.

Buddy left my folding chair perch right where it was. I sit and settle in. My attention wanders and I follow it. On the other side of the fence is the private road that encircles the whole campus, and beyond that a nothing-looking slope leading up to a corridor of trees abutting train tracks. In the middle of the slope, I noticed movement high up on a utility pole. Then I hear squawking. Two bigger-size birds, smaller than a pigeon and larger than a finch, are flying at a raven, perched on the top of the pole.

This utility pole has two crossbeams, that rectangular piece of wood bolted on poles used to hold up power lines. One of the birds flies down to the lower crossbeam, close to where it's bolted to the pole. And then I noticed, tucked into that right angle, a nest. The raven is trying to eat the eggs.

I open my Merlin ID app, the equivalent of Shazam for birds, and press the record button. It identifies the two birds as Cassin's kingbirds, who were living up to their given scientific name of *Tyrannus vociferans,* vociferous tyrant. Eventually, the raven flies away with a croak.

The Merlin ID app heard other birds too, some of whom I did not hear at all:

Say's Phoebe
song sparrow
roadrunner
western bluebird
hummingbird species
American crow
raven
red-tailed hawk

In an instant, the dismal, derelict campus leapt from lifeless to living.

This ugly place will become one of my "patches," a birding term connoting a local spot, a place close to home so that you can go frequently enough to get to know the birds that live there. Patches show me how a seemingly static place is always full of motion.

And even though it would seem that the finches' rejection of the nest box is a negative thing, something lacking motion, it is not. It is still a process, in that something is moving forward, just not in the way I wanted it to. The likelihood of them finding a suitable nesting site was high. I had a sense when I was setting up house that it wasn't the right design. In retrospect, I realized that all the house finch nest sites I'd encountered were more open, like a carport instead of a garage. But I didn't readily know how to build one, nor did I have the tools or time. So I barreled ahead and lurched into the experiment. Sometimes I think if I pause too long, I'll lose momentum. Or maybe I'm just impatient.

Part of what moved forward, besides the finches finding another location to nest, was my understanding of house finches specifically and me more generally. I could have just chalked the so-called failed nest experiment up to an "Oh well, I tried." But I would have shortchanged myself by tossing the experience behind me.

First, if I cared about those finches, then shouldn't I walk the talk by following through with wondering, "Well then, where in the hell *did* they nest?"

And why? What was it about the site they eventually chose and the one they didn't?

The nest box I bought was specifically designed for the eastern bluebird, a species that nests solely in cavities, like a woodpecker hole in a dead tree. Finches do not nest in a cavity, that is, a sheltered chamber; they make a cup nest placed in vegetation or on human-made structures. They are what's known as open nesters. Birds, like us, are not one size fits all. It reminds me of what the acting teacher I mentioned earlier said: "General is the death of acting. Specific. You have to make it specific!"

When you look up the word origin for *specific* or *species* in Merriam-Webster's Collegiate Dictionary, it says, "See *special.*" And that door opens up to *species,* a sort, a kind. You could say, everything is special because everything is a kind. It doesn't mean there's no discernment regarding the value of the special thing, it just means everything is a kind and needs to be regarded as such.

A finch is a kind of bird. A bluebird is a kind of bird. The character I play in the show in New Mexico is a kind of person, and the last character I played is a kind of person. Each needs to be related to specifically. And that takes energy.

THE LITTLE HABITAT behind the trailers has been thriving for almost two months. I am on my way to refill the bird feeder but stopped short. The feeder is already filled.

I don't understand. I knew I hadn't filled it, but it's filled to the brim. I look around as if the answer is nearby, but there's no one in sight.

Yet clearly someone noticed this little area and wanted to be a part of it. They took the time to buy birdseed and fill the feeder. And now I feel a part of that. I don't know who it was, but I'm not alone.

Next to the nest box, hanging from the chain-link fence, I see a lunch box–sized, handmade house with a diorama inside depicting beautifully drawn birds.

These mysterious art projects continued to grow; the patch of chain-link fence transformed into a cabinet of curiosities. The actual nest box remained empty, but the area did not. It is filled with birds drinking and eating and now miniature handmade houses, with drawings of birds inside. I don't know who made these additions, and it's okay. It's a fellow human being, now part of this ecosystem of living things continually interacting with the environment.

ONE DAY IN JULY, a couple of weeks before we wrap, I am walking from my trailer to the stages when a woman stops me and says, "I'm the one who's been filling your bird feeder. I work in the art department."

I pull her into me and give her a huge hug. After a long embrace, I smile and look at her. We are comfortable without the words. We know we're connected. We share a bond, a connection to the living things around us.

On the last day of shooting, I don't pack up the bird feeder, nest box, and birdbath but leave them right where they are. They will most likely stay empty, short of the birdbath filling with a bit of rainwater—but they might not. I've set up bird feeders in almost every place I've stayed for an extended period of time, and I always feel a pang of guilt for abandoning them when I return to my own home.

My guilt has been lessened by some solid research showing that birds do not become dependent on bird feeders. Several studies show that if bird feeders suddenly disappear, birds will seamlessly move to a natural resource. But scientists are also finding that little patches of habitat in critically important areas can make the difference between life or death, especially during migration, when fuel is crucial.

You don't have to do much to get a lot in the natural world. If you provide, they will come. The animals will come. And the people will come too, in the sense that our empathy or curiosity will arrive once the animal does, if we notice it. If we pay attention, it is there for the taking.

9

Catbird

I had just started rehearsals for a Broadway play, and I was going to be working in the Times Square area from May to middle August.

For most New Yorkers, Times Square can be a kind of hell. The senses are bombarded with massive digital screens and billboards, moving lights, honking, yelling, music, sirens. The throngs of visitors, lacking the city sense of people-navigation, can thwart even a "New York minute" walker like me.

Thankfully, my subway stop was on Sixth Avenue and Forty-second Street, a block east of the district, so I wasn't immediately thrust into the chaos. But that junction is also a hustle-bustling place, though not as intense as Times Square.

One day in the first week of rehearsal, as I climbed from the underground subway up into the world, I realized I had forty-five minutes to kill.

Bryant Park was to my right, a blur of green as I hurried past. I told myself to slow down and wait a minute, but I didn't feel like listening. I told myself it's a beautiful park. Why not go in? John Muir, the father of national parks, said the clearest way into the universe is through a forest. I'd had enough experience to know that that forest can be Bryant Park. That forest can be your backyard, a fire escape, an abandoned lot. And I'd heard there was a catbird in Bryant Park from BirdsEye, the bird-finding app that tells you what birds are nearby. Why not have a small adventure before rehearsal?

Roughly twenty steps after I enter the park, my resistance started falling away and my step had a new pep to it. I crossed over what felt like a threshold despite myself and was eager to find the catbird.

Now, I've seen a catbird before, many times. I know a catbird. It's a common bird, a little smaller than a robin, slate gray with a clean black cap, a splash of rufous under the tail. It's in the Mimid family along with the mockingbird and brown thrasher. The catbird makes a variety of musical and harsh sounds as well as a catlike mewing. It's not a rarity in the city, and some birders might say, "You're looking for a catbird? Why?"

Any bird that isn't a pigeon or a house sparrow, living in the heart of a metropolis, is worth visiting. Some pigeon lovers say pigeons are too. I'm working on that.

As I scanned the park, I was confident and convinced I was going to see the catbird—so much so, I was strutting around like John Travolta from *Saturday Night Fever,* looking here, looking there, strutting on. But my strut lost its confidence the longer I looked. It started to dawn on me that I didn't know the catbird at all. I knew it made the mewing sound, I knew it was gray and had a black hat, but I didn't know how it behaved, what it ate, if it liked the ground or the high trees. I felt overwhelmed. The park suddenly felt loud, the volume knob turned up high. There was a lot going on. I didn't know where to start. The place felt enormous and general.

I wanted to leave. This wasn't relaxing. It didn't feel good. But I kept walking. I told myself to just walk slowly. Follow your feet. Don't think.

I found myself stopped in front of a leaf at eye level. I didn't have any idea what it was. I'd been classifying leaves just as Green Things, but what was it? What's its purpose? Is it from here? Is it a food source?

I had just discovered the app iNaturalist. You take a photo of any plant, animal, insect, any living thing, you upload it to a community of almost a million expert and novice naturalists, and they help you name it. They say this leaf in front of me is named viburnum. It's native, meaning that it belongs here. I feel better knowing something; there is one less stranger in the world. I stay with my new friend viburnum and scan the ground it's rooted in. I walk alongside the row of plantings like a detective, looking carefully, pausing, continuing. Out of the corner of my eye I see a guy sitting on a bench, looking at me with his head slight cocked, eyes squinting. I employ my acting skills and pretend I lost something. I touch my ear, feeling for the ghost earring, hoping he picks up on that. I wish I wasn't so self-conscious.

I resume honest looking when I'm out of his view. But my

energy is dipping. I'm not making any progress at all. But then I ask, is it really about finding this one thing? Isn't it also about being in the moment and not worrying about the goal? Yeah. But I also wanted to find the goddamn catbird.

As I continue walking, I'm acutely aware of inner tumult: defenses, protestations, resistances, and the countering psychological gymnastics to work through them. Surrender never comes out of peace. I noticed how restricted my view was. I tried to keep my eyes soft, like a gaze. I'd read about that in a book on wildlife tracking: something about a soft gaze so you can take in everything while keeping a focus, but not in a myopic way so that you can't see anything else. The effect is immediate because there's a tangible thing to work with; soften the eyes, stay alert. I started to get the hang of it; my perception changed. The ache from holding on too tight was gone.

I saw movement in the bushes; a leaf moved in a different way. A pattern break.

I'm always delighted when I experience how good humans are at noticing pattern breaks. It's kind of what we're designed for. If we weren't so good at it, we would have been eaten long ago by the animals on the ancient savannah. One pattern break I love to observe is when there's a rat on the subway tracks. When I notice the rat, I look around quickly to see if anyone else has. Inevitably I find another human staring beady-eyed at the interloper and I smile.

I look back at the rat, see it scurry, look back at the platform, and catch another human newly alert to the situation. That person's focus, itself a sort of pattern break, alerts someone nearby to focus on what their neighbor is looking at. Soon maybe half the people around me have noticed the rat. There may be some who noticed it but didn't show it because some New Yorkers aren't fazed by anything.

I stop at attention in front of the bush with the leaf that moved. So as not to disturb the living thing in the bush, I moved carefully, economically, as if I'm balancing a glass on my head. I wait. I see a different leaf move in the bush next door. My eyes move from the leaf to another movement, a flash of gray. The catbird. I got it. Bullseye. Jackpot. I'm done. I'm tired. I can go. But what the hell. What's that about? I ask myself to observe it. I admitted earlier, practically out loud, that I didn't know anything about the catbird. Here's an opportunity to learn in real life, from the source, not a book or an app—and if for nothing else, to at least recognize this catbird for surviving the park. It's moving among all these human beings, sounds. What's it like for this catbird living in here? What does it eat in this park? I hadn't thought much about what birds eat besides bird seed.

It hops onto the ground, which has small bits of trash smushed into it. It pecks at a crumpled strip of plastic, tosses it back to the ground. It continues hopping underneath the bushes, hops up to a branch, and pecks at something. It looks around. I feel like I'm in the bush with the catbird, tranquil, the cacophonous park sounds recede. I squat down and look at the soil, a beetle crawling. The vibrant green of the leaves.

Only when I was out of the park and a block away from the rehearsal space did I take in how good it felt.

There is a universe in Bryant Park that I can tap into whenever I want.

After rehearsal that day, as I approached the stairs to the subway, the park was no longer a green blur. I knew two things in that park now: the catbird, the viburnum. I descended the steps, about to be transported to another place, Brooklyn. As I waited for the train, standing directly underneath the park, maybe even under the catbird, I felt steady on the ground beneath me and aware of the ground above me.

As with any relationship, the park and I had ebbs and flows. Familiarity breeds contempt but only if you think you know the thing that's familiar. The ebbs might be a drag but they're not contemptible; without the ebb there would be no flow.

The park became very familiar because I passed it twice a day, six days a week for four months. The typical theater schedule is eight shows a week: two shows on Wednesday, two on Saturday. Sunday is a matinee and Monday is off. I didn't go into the park every day, but it was in my consciousness. I could tune into it as if it were a radio station.

The catbird isn't the only bird in Bryant Park. Since data was first collected, on January 5, 1979, a total of 144 species of birds have passed through the park. That is all the different kinds of birds, not individuals. In spring and fall that number can jump to more than forty species. But I noticed by the end of May a lot of the other birds had migrated on; they were like tourists. The catbird like a resident. Catbirds breed in the park, and though some take off around November after the young are grown, many hardy ones also stay through the winter.

Until early June, I saw only that one catbird. There was an intimacy in focusing on that individual. One late afternoon, I saw some stagehand-type people dressed in black, working on things related to a show: setting up a stage, speakers, chairs. There was a sound check. It was really loud. I imagined people streaming into the park. I thought of the disruption to the living creatures that call the park home. Their environment was constantly being invaded by human events: a skating rink, concerts, fashion week.

I kept thinking of the catbird throughout the evening, imagining it trying to sleep through all the noise. I looked for it the next day, and there it was, hopping on the ground under the protective shrubs—another day in paradise.

It was around the beginning of June that I saw the catbird fly into an English plane tree and then saw a second catbird fly into the same spot. Then one flew out and swooped into a shrub. The second one followed with a stick in its beak. Nest building. Life begins.

As the preparation for new life was under way in Bryant Park I was settling into the run of the show. Performing in a play creates an interesting schedule. You're going off to work, late afternoon or early evening, when everyone else is going home. You get home late when everyone is in bed and get to bed even later because it takes time to wind down from the show. You wake up later than everyone else and then have the day free, but it doesn't feel free because a part of you is connected, absorbed with the play. I liken the experience of performing in a play to a runner's training for a marathon. But the actor has a race every night, and the day is spent readying for the race. Each race is part of a greater marathon that is the entire run of the show from opening to closing night.

What works best during the day of the show are activities that require some of you but not all of you, a state of mind like the "soft gaze" I mentioned earlier.

The perfect place to direct that gaze was on the "green things" in my backyard. My Brooklyn apartment is on the second floor of a brownstone composed of four units with a shared backyard. I had set up a bird feeder and a birdbath out back, but many of the plants had been there forever and were unknown to me. Since knowing that viburnum leaf in Bryant Park, I wasn't able to look at any living green thing in the same way. Consciousness is like that; once the door is opened, the light shines in on everything related to the subject that nudged the door open.

I had been hearing about native plants for a few years, but the soil hadn't been fertile enough for the seed to take. Now that it was, I found my way to an important book, *Bringing Nature Home.* It's not a how-to book. It's a how-come book.

The author, Doug Tallamy, is an entomologist, with a primary focus on Lepidoptera: butterflies and moths. Early in his scientific research, he discovered the connection between caterpillars and birds. Caterpillars, of course, are those fuzzy worm-looking things with legs that turn into butterflies and moths. He soon realized that birds depended on those caterpillars during the breeding season as a food source for their chicks. Caterpillars are energy rich, high in protein and fats that nestlings need to grow and develop. It's estimated that one nestling needs hundreds to thousands of caterpillars to survive. He also found that the birds preferred feeding their young with native caterpillars rather than non-native ones. Through a coevolutionary process taking place over thousands of years, caterpillars learned how to adapt to the chemical protective mechanisms that plants used to make them less tasty. In turn, the caterpillars were able to convert the healthy chemical compounds needed for their survival into energy. Tallamy's research showed that caterpillars transfer more energy from plants to other animals than any other plant-eating creature. So what plants were the best for caterpillars and thus best for birds? Tallamy says the number one most productive plant in North America is the oak tree. More than nine hundred species of Lepidoptera use oaks. The yard was small so I couldn't plant an oak tree, but there were excellent runners-up.

As I entered into the kingdom Plantea, in my little Brooklyn patch, I was delighted to discover that I had beneficial natives in the yard: horseweed, snakeroot, pokeweed, Pennsylvania pellitory, fleabane. Some of the plants were no good:

crabgrass, Oriental bittersweet, buckthorn. They were "invasive species," non-native species that can cause ecological and environmental harm.

I took time developing the list of plants for my backyard. I realized I was creating an ecosystem—a diverse system that would provide life for other life forms.

I looked more carefully at the plantings in Bryant Park, because whoever planned it was thinking along the same lines. Not only did the catbirds find food on the viburnum but they also used it as a habitat. The nest they built was buried deep within the shrub, staying true to their scientific genus, *Dumetella,* meaning "small thicket."

The female was brooding and the male was guarding, the energy contained and inward. She would incubate the eggs for twelve to fourteen days. I knew the eggs had hatched because the brooding energy turned animated. The adults flew in with food and out to find more. Bryant Park was providing what they needed. While the catbirds were feeding the nestlings, I finalized my list of plants: joe-pye weed, viburnum, chokecherry, lobelia, and a dogwood tree.

I went to Lowe's to find some plants. I had a feeling I wouldn't find them all, but I thought there'd be one or two to get started. None. Not one native plant. I went to a nursery thinking that because it wasn't multitasking like Lowe's it would deliver. Not one native. I went to another nursery. After browsing for a good twenty minutes, I found one native plant.

The nurseries started to feel eerie, like the plants were Stepford wives: pretty, vacant, and lacking life. There were no insects at these nurseries. No pollinators, no bees. All the nurseries were stocked with a brand of plant called Proven Winners. Most aren't from here or they're what's called a *hybrid,* a plant created by crossbreeding different varieties of plants, and not a single insect was on them. Winners for whom? I'd never considered any of this when buying plants in the past. I'd just bought what looked nice.

I had to order the native plants from two different online nurseries that specialize in natives. Native plants sell out fast, probably because there are so few places to get them, and many weren't available, or I had to wait for them to get back in stock.

As the Bryant Park catbird nestlings approached fledging, each day felt like opening a door to an Advent calendar with a question mark on the door of the big day.

On a Friday around 5:00 p.m. before the show, I dropped into the park to open that day's calendar door. The parents were not near the nest. I walked along the row of plantings near the nest, sticking my nose into the shrubs, squatting down to get a lower view. I wasn't finding anything. I looked on the opposite side of the path. I went back up on the original side.

Then I saw, deep in a bush, a small, fluffy bird shaking its feathers. Above it was another fluffy bird. They had that open-eyed, bewildered look of nestlings.

The adults were nearby at different station posts, keeping a watchful eye. The fledglings looked healthy. On day one out of the nest, they were experiencing the full city life. The weekend was approaching, and I was sure there'd be events in the park. They will adjust and adapt over time, just like the adults. Something is working in this habitat.

My plants arrived and I took them out of their boxes, but then I got caught up with something, and then something else. The plants sat on the small brick patio adjacent to the yard. I knew I was procrastinating but kept pushing the task away.

One day I was looking out the window into the backyard, as I often do, passing by to peek at what's going on (there's always something going on). I saw the plants awaiting their planting and felt guilty. Then I saw a monarch butterfly wafting over the neighboring backyards. It landed on a plant but didn't stay long because there was nothing for it there. It stopped at another plant and moved on. It kept doing this, floating from one plant to another.

When I'm moved, often my nose hurts, and then I get a welling up in my eyes. The monarch was on its way back to Mexico, flying endlessly in search of food. If it didn't find food that day, would it flutter to the ground and die? How long could it go without food?

I sped down the stairs to the outside. I grabbed a shovel and the joe-pye weed, one of the monarch's favorite foods. As I dug the hole, I looked up intermittently to see if the monarch was still around. I put the joe-pye weed in the ground and filled in the hole with dirt. I sat on the grass, my body tense as I prayed for the monarch to come back.

The monarch wafted over and touched gently down in the middle of a bulbous mass of purple flowers. The monarch feeds on the joe-pye weed and many other native plants, but the only plant they can lay their eggs on is the milkweed plant. And the monarch caterpillar feeds exclusively on milkweed leaves.

I took a photo of that monarch on the joe-pye weed. I also took a photo of the first catbird I saw in Bryant Park and the two juvenile catbirds in the bush. I looked back at those photos when writing this chapter.

Sometimes when we have big shifts in our consciousness it's hard to detect when it happened or how it happened. It's sort of like if someone were to ask what you were thinking the moment before you woke up.

I hadn't fully appreciated the significance the catbird played in catalyzing a chain of connections. Before the catbird photo, there were flashes of green as I scrolled back through the mosaic of photos on my phone. But after the catbird photo, those flashes had burst into a sea of green. Hundreds and hundreds of photos taken of unknown and unnamed plants, shared with the iNaturalist community. Each leaf, flower, insect eventually named and known.

All the green things around me are now somethings. I know I can stand anywhere among living things, connected to things that are connected to other things. I'm in a net holding me to the catbird, to the viburnum, the caterpillar, the butterfly, the sun.

10

Sparrow

One summer, I got involved in a war between some bluebirds and a house sparrow. It got so ugly I went and bought a pellet gun at DICK'S Sporting Goods. I sat in a low-to-the-ground lawn chair with the gun across my lap, keeping watch on those bluebirds like an obsessive Ma Kettle. I eventually put the pellet gun away because it's impossible to shoot if your target is more than five inches away, as mine, the sparrow, was. Little did I know we'd need another kind of gun.

Passer domesticus. House sparrow. Stealer of houses. That ubiquitous little brown and white bird flitting about in suburbs and cities throughout the United States. In New York City, they are one of two birds you can count on seeing almost anywhere, along with the pigeon. And like the pigeon, they aren't shy. They readily frequent the feeder and don't flee when you approach the window to watch them.

Over the years, at the feeders at my various New York City apartments, I watched them.

They weren't very nice to each other: always bickering,

kicking one another off the perches at the feeding ports, sometimes wrestling in the dirt. I thought I was noticing them, but now that I know what that means, I wasn't.

I accepted them because I didn't know there was anything better out there. They were a glimmer of light through the window slat in a prison cell in the days before I entered the world of birds.

I understand now that they were satisfying an innate hunger—a hunger or yearning that, I believe, isn't specific to me or to birds. E. O. Wilson believes that we all have within us an intrinsic capacity to respond to nature. Birds are my gateway into that innate capacity. For some it's sunsets, clouds, trees, butterflies, stars, or just being outside grilling at the barbecue and taking in the beauty while the meat cooks.

"When did you start to like birds?"

I get asked that question a lot, and it's hard for me to answer because it didn't happen in one fell swoop, so to speak. It was gradual *and* sudden, like a sunrise. I always knew birds were there. I was aware of them. But I didn't know them or notice them in the true sense of that word; the root of *notice* is "to know."

I'm realizing now that the sparrow did in fact, spark something, but I never thought of it as my "spark bird" because that term connotes positive associations. I won't go so far as to grant it the title of "spark bird," but I do owe the sparrow a debt of gratitude.

Before that summer of the warring sparrow, I was in a fairy

tale. The sparrow played the part of the evil witch, presenting obstacles that I needed to overcome to cross the threshold from innocence to knowingness.

I NOTICED SOME sweet blue birds in my yard, at my house in upstate New York. I had never seen a blue like that in real life, a flying gem, flashing ultramarine blue. They reminded me of the cute blue birds in the Disney cartoons, particularly the classic *Sleeping Beauty,* one of my favorite movies when I was little. Princess Aurora, aka Sleeping Beauty, sang a song, "I Wonder," to the little birds when she was in the forest, and when the song was over, the little birds tweeted shyly, batted their eyes, and nestled on her shoulder.

I don't know what the species of the blue birds in *Sleeping Beauty* was, but I learned what was in my yard: the eastern bluebird.

Then I discovered a book, *The Bluebird Monitor's Guide to Bluebirds and Other Small Cavity Nesters.* Reading through the book felt like a serious teacher was commanding me to pay attention, so I did. The book laid out everything from how to build a nest box to removing blowflies off a baby chick.

Bluebirds can't nest just anywhere. They are what's called "obligate secondary cavity nesters"; they must nest in a cavity, but they don't actually make the cavity, hence the word *secondary.* Birds such as woodpeckers create the cavity, which is simply a chamber with an entrance that shelters the nest and eggs. Sparrows prefer cavities, but unlike the bluebird, they can nest almost anywhere, and some have even been known to excavate the cavity themselves.

House sparrows aren't native to North America and didn't fly here on their own volition; they most likely sailed on a ship, carried in a cage by some European person. Once they were here, they wanted the same cavities that the bluebirds had been using for thousands and thousands of years. They were bigger and stronger, kind of like guns versus a bow and arrow. By the 1920s, bluebird numbers had declined by 90 percent, simply because they weren't making little bluebirds.

In 1926, Thomas Musselman of Illinois came up with the idea of creating a trail of bluebird nest boxes that people could monitor, like a Secret Service for the bluebird. The idea took off, and by the 1970s the bluebird was on its way to a healthy recovery. Today there are multiple organizations dedicated to them: the North American Bluebird Society covers the United States, but many states have their own chapter, like my own state's New York State Bluebird Society.

Being restless and impatient, I didn't build a house from scratch but opted for the premade nest box, approved by the North American Bluebird Society, with the primary specifications of a circular hole no larger than one and a half inches (to keep sparrows and starlings out) and a side of the house that can be lifted for monitoring. Any box not officially approved can be a "deathtrap."

The nest box needs to be mounted on a square post or circular pole, situated away from anything that gives a predator easy access into the box, say a tree branch just above it. The solution to stopping predators from the ground up is a cylindrical apparatus, called a baffler or predator guard, that fits around the post or pole, in effect thwarting a predator like a raccoon, cat, snake, squirrel, or chipmunk. The bluebird faces many threats and challenges, but the sparrow is enemy number one. I skipped over the sparrow stuff in the book because I didn't have sparrows on my land. I had no idea why. I hadn't thought much about it.

The nest box was up by the middle of March, but no bluebirds seemed to want it. I would visit the nest box daily, lift the side panel, peek inside: no nest material, no bird, no nothing.

And then one day, with expectations worn down, I went to lift the panel and was greeted not by emptiness but by three pieces of dried grass stems.

I didn't know the bluebirds were still around. I thought they had moved on to a nest box mounted by someone who knew what they were doing.

I expected the grass to form quickly into a nest, but things moved at a pace I didn't understand. The pieces of grass just sat, for days and days, taking on the character of tumbleweed. I didn't understand what the problem was; they'd signed the lease, why weren't they moving in? Chop, chop. We humans don't dilly-dally around like that. Once we seal the deal, we get the contractors in and call the movers.

Then, suddenly one day, there were more pieces of dried grass and soon a few more, gradually becoming a clump. But I never saw the birds bring it; they were like elves slipping in and out when my back was turned. The pieces of dried grass increased, uniting into a nest.

The nest remained empty for days, another small mystery, and then, on one of my daily checks, I lifted the side panel, and my eye met the eye of the female bluebird on the nest, body tense. Her eyes widened, but she stayed. I gently closed the panel and crept away, finding a secretive place to observe.

Once the coast was clear—from me—I saw the male bluebird take off from a lower branch on a large pin oak tree, about twenty-five feet from the nest box. He flew down quickly, grabbed something in his beak, then flew directly into the nest box. Maybe he was feeding her while she stayed on the nest. But then later in the day, I saw her leave. He was gone too. I quickly looked in the box to check for eggs. Empty. I placed my hand gently in the nest and it was warm.

I felt like an undercover spy, clocking their moves, executing covert operations when it was safe. She was in the nest box most of the time. After a few days of not being able to check, I finally had my chance. Four blue eggs. Warm. During the incubation stage, in order not to stress her out, I would no longer check inside the box unless there was an emergency.

The nest box reminded me of an ancient Sanskrit prayer. The beginning goes like this:

Look to this day
for it is life
the very life of life.
In its brief course lie all
the realities and truths of existence.

EVENTUALLY, the eggs hatched. On day one, there were four pink, orange, and jaundice-colored alien-like creatures no bigger than one and a half inches, with tufts of gray hairs on what looked like a head and dark gray bulbous disks on either side of a yellow beak.

On day two, tufts of hair sprouted on the back of "arms" that looked to be missing hands, and short thighs with long feet. I couldn't help but think of a very sick old man.

By day five, the beaks looked less like the odd nose of a proboscis monkey. On the funny-looking arms, what looked like gray-blue bruises, I learned, were the tips of pin feathers; they appeared like a pin poking through the skin. They are also called blood feathers. While the feather grows, it requires a blood supply to nourish it. A sheath made of keratin covers the growing feather, protecting it until it is fully grown. Then the sheath falls away, and the blood recedes to the base of the feather. The chicks were still too young for me to pick up and check. I discovered a wasp was in the top corner of the box, probably wanting to also build a nest. I grabbed the wasp with a paper towel, then smushed it.

Day eight and their eyes were open. They shifted from alien to bird. Pin feathers continued to grow, now covering the head fully, the wings, the center of the back. The sides of the back were still bald.

On day eleven, I saw blowflies in the nest material. I needed to inspect each chick. One had blowfly larvae under the wing, little gross black blobs. Blowfly larvae, the babies of blowflies, were also trying to live, albeit parasitically, off the blood of the chick. The larvae wouldn't directly kill the chick but could weaken it, which could lead to death. I pulled off the creepy blowflies and returned the nestling.

Day thirteen was my last day of opening the nest box. Fledging usually occurs between days fifteen and eighteen. When the chicks are close to fledging, there's a danger when opening the box that they will fly out before they're ready.

I lifted each chick out one more time. This time I'd verify the sexes: bright blue wingtips for males, dull blue gray for females.

They looked like real, adult birds now except for the fluffy raggedness, the uncoordinated movements, and the need to still nestle in with each other. Adult birds don't do that because they are not nestlings.

As I sat and waited for the chicks to fledge, I wondered what it might be like in that box. The chicks were getting bigger. They had wings they wanted to use.

Scientists have discovered that caged birds display the same restlessness as their counterparts in the wild at the onset of migration. This inborn urge to move is called *zugunruhe,* a German word meaning simply "move" and "restlessness."

The word refers primarily to migration but also to that deep urge to move that is in every living thing: a need to move forward, on, toward, and conversely a deep restlessness when trapped, stuck, or static. The saying "Nature abhors a vacuum" has been on our minds since Aristotle came up with it in 1 BCE. A vacuum is emptiness, and maybe it's the emptiness nature doesn't like. Something that's empty is closed; it doesn't have anything coming in, no new energy moving toward something.

On day sixteen, a chick's scrappy head peeked out of the hole, then disappeared. Hours later, it reappeared, staying longer than the first time. Soon, the chick was always at the hole—not watching, not waiting, but readying. I spaced out, distracted by something. I looked back, and the hole was empty. I scanned the surroundings and located the fledgling in the pin oak tree, shaking its feathers. Another chick soon appeared at the hole. I dedicated time to watching, pushing other things to the back burner. I wanted to see this one fledge. I wanted to see the moment it leapt into the unknown.

Its head pushed outside the hole. It was trying to get up higher, most likely scrambling on the backs of its siblings to secure a sturdier foothold for takeoff.

Without any trumpets or cheers, it flew to the pin oak, fluffed its feathers, and looked around. Momentous events happen quietly, without fanfare. If you came upon that small bird, not knowing anything, you would think it had been out in the world forever.

Later that day, the third one fledged. I didn't see it happen, but I saw three bluebirds in the pin oak tree with a bewildered quality and knew.

I thought of that fourth chick. All its siblings were gone. Would it have the oomph to get out? Probably, but how uncomfortable to still be in there.

Its head popped up. No one was cheering it on. The parents were busy feeding the three on the outside. Maybe they didn't feed the one in the box anymore. Maybe it was tough love time. The siblings were thrilled to be out and didn't want to look back. The chick was on its own. Purgatory or life.

Three hours before sunset, the chick fledged.

WHAT HAD BEEN a humming, thriving, living world was now a ghost town. I opened the side panel for what would be the last time. The walls were lightly whitewashed with excrement; the edge of the nest's original cup shape created to contain the chicks had been smushed down; little bits of undigested berries, seeds, and bugs littered the once-pristine, cozy nest bed. The whole thing had a "get out of Dodge" feel. And I wanted to get out too. This box was in the past. It was over. The life was out there now. But was there a way to give some thanks, close the door gently instead of slamming it shut? The old nest box was gross, but it wasn't ugly. The chicks hadn't fled because the place was a shithole. They had left right on time.

If they had stayed, then the nest box would have been ugly—a house of morbid, stuck energy. A place to flee from.

That was my first brood of bluebirds. I continued to monitor over the course of three breeding seasons, which means three years. The fourth year of monitoring, a sparrow came to town.

Prior to that, I hadn't seen any on my land. They've adapted exceptionally well to being around humans, and my house was located in a more rural setting, not their favorite habitat. What changed was that my neighbor had begun raising chickens, and I think it was the copious amount of feed that brought them in.

When that sparrow entered the scene, I had two nest boxes up. One was occupied by a pair of bluebirds in the process of raising four chicks; the second box was empty. The chicks were thirteen days old, and it was going to be my final check. As I approached the box, something didn't feel right. It was too quiet.

I opened the side door: four nestlings dead, their eyes gouged out, bodies crumpled.

It felt malicious and cruel, but a human hadn't done it. Some animal had, and they don't have malice; they don't consciously do evil.

I scanned the area; the sweet, bucolic setting, once safe and serene, was now sinister, menacing. I heard a harsh sound, jackhammering the air, a staccato chirp, chirp, chirp, chirp. I walked away from the death box, searching for that awful sound.

And then I saw it. The sparrow, perched on a fence, shouting into the world.

I tipped into the chasm between fight or flight—an interesting experience when facing off with a bird. I went into fight. I ran top speed straight at him. He saw me running and flew. That running was an irrational move, ineffectual. I took a breath and tried to think straight. I saw him on a tree branch near the second box, the unoccupied one. I stayed put, wanting to be smarter moving forward. I waited and watched. He flew into the second nest box. So much for the special one-and-a-half-inch hole meant to keep sparrows out.

Losing control again, I ran to the nest box and jerked the side panel up, hoping to scare him, which I did. He flew out fast. Inside, there was a nest: sloppy, messy, nothing like the elegant, neat bluebird nest. I yanked it out and threw it to the ground, slamming the door shut.

I sat down on the ground and waited. I'm not sure for what. It felt better to stay near the danger. He flew back in from wherever he had gone and landed on the fence rail, fifty feet from the nest box. So much for scaring him.

He flew down off the railing and landed sideways on a long stem of grass. Unsteadily swaying back and forth, he broke off a piece, about five inches long. Material in beak, he flew back into the nest box.

He flew back out, U-turned, and landed on the roof of the house. Standing tall and proud, he chirped incessantly. He noticed the male bluebird on the roof of the other nest box and flew straight at him.

I ran into the house and flipped open my computer. We'd been invaded. The enemy was here. I went straight to Sialis .org, a bluebird website. But this time I went to the section on house sparrows, which I had previously sashayed past. The section began with a warning: "This webpage deals with both active and passive means of managing House Sparrow (HOSP) populations. House Sparrows are deadly and difficult, but there are ways to manage them."

I'm in. I pledge. I accept.

Below the warning, there was a quote:

> Without question, the most deplorable event in the history of American ornithology was the introduction of the English Sparrow.
>
> —W. L. Dawson, *The Birds of Ohio,* 1903.

Someone on the outside might think the quote over the top, hyperbolic, even silly. That's your big gripe? Out of all the terrible things in the world, you land on the house sparrow?

But because I now carried the image of the dead baby bluebirds and the confused adults, W. L. Dawson's pronouncement soothed me, mirroring the intense hatred I had for that sparrow and, more importantly, letting me know I wasn't alone.

My first sane question was how to get the sparrow to stop building a nest.

Within moments, I arrived at the answer.

You don't.

The author says, you let them build, because they won't stop. No matter what. But fear not, the author of this site tells me, there is a solution.

I would let them build a nest; I would let the female lay her eggs. As I waited for their sloppy nest building to finish, waited for her to lay the eggs, I would stroll by the nest nonchalantly, like a cartoon character walking past whistling an "I don't care, don't mind me" tune. My act might have bombed on stage, but the male sparrow was buying it; he seemed totally unperturbed by my presence.

The eggs were laid. I waited for the moment when both parents were gone from the nest, then I carefully removed the eggs and brought them to the kitchen, where a pot of water was boiling. I gently spooned each individual egg into the boiling water, setting the timer for four minutes. I removed them, let them cool and returned them to the nest. The hope was that the female would sit and sit on the eggs but because they'd been cooked (in other words, they were duds), they wouldn't hatch.

There was a high probability she would get spooked and the pair would abandon the nest completely and move away.

A current of manic energy ran through me, enjoyable if I didn't pause too long to sense the crash at the end of the road.

I relished stealing the eggs, boiling them, returning them cold. I felt relief, as I imagined her sitting on the duds, that this nightmare might soon end.

While the female sparrow was pseudo-incubating, the male sparrow continued to harass the pair of bluebirds, whose offspring he massacred, as they attempted to build a new nest. The house sparrow was like a greedy child, his toys scattered over the playground, dashing back and forth, striking anyone who touched them.

I felt uneasy about the length of time the female sparrow was taking incubating the dud eggs. I lifted the panel, not caring that I scared her off the nest. One of the boiled eggs had hatched.

The Terminator sparrow was born.

I admire generals. I could never be one. It is so far from my reality; I don't understand what a general's mind is like. But I needed to think like one, exercise that underdeveloped part of me: clear decision-making, keeping emotions in check, logic.

I needed to adapt, confront, explore difficult options; I needed to move from passive to active control of the house sparrow. That image of the four dead baby bluebirds and two lost adults helped focus me.

I BOUGHT A TRAPDOOR apparatus to trap sparrows; a square metal plate with a spring-loaded mechanism that you mount on the inside of the box. When the sparrow flies in, it trips the mechanism, and a plate covers up the hole. But it didn't work. He flew in and out, each time evading the mechanism. I tried to manually trap him, by attaching a long string to the trap door, and yanking it shut once he went in, but my yanking speed was too slow; he was long gone by the time I shut it. Once the string got tangled around a stick on the ground. I felt like he was laughing at me.

I set up a Havahart trap even though I felt heartless, but another species of sparrow, the song sparrow, native to the United States, got caught in the trapdoor and died.

I got a pellet gun from DICK'S Sporting Goods store, sat in a low camouflaged hunting chair, and waited. But the sparrow wouldn't approach because I was too close. I had to move back ten feet, twenty feet. When I was forty feet back, the sparrow finally approached the box. I took aim and fired a shot. My aim was ridiculous: the pellet went nowhere near the sparrow. Impossible. I rewatched the YouTube video of a guy shooting a target on the ground with a pellet gun and noticed that his shoes were in the video—he was only six inches away. I hadn't caught that the first time I watched. That's when I discovered the pellet gun only works when you're right next to your target. I abandoned the gun.

The end of summer was nearing. The Terminator son was grown now; soon, he'd be taking after his father.

I was obsessed, and it was wearing me down; my sole focus was that sparrow. During conversations, I had one ear tuned to his sounds, my vision widened out to catch his movements. The bluebird pair were still around but had given up on the nest box. I felt responsible for their lack of procreating. I had enticed them to nest by putting up that box and then had failed to protect their raison d'être: to make life.

I felt trapped by an unrelenting, small-ass killer. The stakes felt too high, like it was life or death, and it was, on a micro level, but my mind had made it macro. I couldn't let it go because there was still a sliver of hope the bluebird pair could make one brood before summer was over. But the few solutions I had left, one being gassing him, were all contingent on catching him.

I threw up the white flag, and in that surrender, space opened up.

My neighbor Mike floated into my mind.

Mike was an older man, in his eighties, and had lived upstate all his life. He liked to hunt, but he especially liked to skeet shoot, where you throw a clay pigeon in the air and shoot it. He made his own bullets. He loved the whole art of it.

Mike liked bluebirds too. I went down the driveway and asked him if he could help me by shooting the sparrow. He said, sure, he'd get his gun and meet me up there. Walking back up the driveway, I felt hopeful, in good hands. I'd been scared and panicky for weeks. I felt like a kid, like the world didn't feel safe. And now a grown-up had just said, "I'll take care of it."

MIKE WALKED UP the driveway with his gun. He asked where the sparrow was. As usual, the bastard was on the fence post, chirping the chirp of death. Mike pulled his gun up to his shoulder, looked carefully, and blew him to smithereens. The enemy was gone.

But then I remembered the Terminator. And then I heard him, chirping in the bushes near where his father had been shot.

When he did come out, he was skittish and wouldn't stay in one place long enough for Mike to take aim. Mike said the bird had gone gun-shy. I now understood that phrase.

I TOOK THE BLUEBIRD boxes down. As long as the sparrow was here, it was unethical to leave the boxes up.

I put them in a far corner of the basement.

That fall, with a bite in the air, brown leaves whispering on the trees, I heard the soft twirly call of the male bluebird. He wasn't looking for a mate because it wasn't breeding season, but he was here and singing.

ON A COLD SPRING DAY, I heard the song again, rusty but renewed. The sorrowful song from the fall was no match for the burst. Nietzsche's sentiment that sorrow is deep but joy is deeper sprang me into action.

Going back to the old nest boxes was not an option. I opened my computer and once again visited the oracle of bluebirds, Sialis.org. The writer of this great site led me to another kind of nest box, specifically designed to keep sparrows out, called the Gilbertson Nest Box, the same size as a regular nest box but made from PVC pipe, painted to look like a birch tree. For whatever reason, sparrows did not like the box at all.

I ordered two, they arrived, and I set to work. The song of the male bluebird provided inspiration and focus.

I put them in a completely different area of the yard. A fresh start.

Finally, by June, a bluebird pair took to one of the boxes. The other box remained empty. The pair had one brood that summer; maybe they wanted to test-run it before expending precious energy.

The Gilbertson Nest Box passed the test. It is the only one I use now. Some years I haven't been able to commit to monitoring, because of time and logistics, but when I can, I do. I've told myself it's nonnegotiable. Hope can't spring eternal if it's stuck.

11

Cranes

As I drove the long, straight road through Nebraska, it felt like I was heading to meet a friend who didn't know I was coming. More like *friends*—upward of five hundred thousand.

When I was invited to visit the sandhill cranes, I said *yes* instead of my default of *no*. And this simple fact made me realize that birds were helping to repair my neural pathways—lifting me up and out from the ruts carved from years of habitual wiring. And like the stork that carries the bundle of hope to its new home, birds were delivering me to unknown places and experiences.

This time I'd been carried to a place where over half a million sandhill cranes stop over during their spring migration, undergoing what's called a staging process, where they gain 20 percent of their body weight to continue their journey to places as far north as Siberia to breed.

Birds need pit stops, just like us when we're on a long road trip. We have multiple opportunities to refill and recharge along the way: gas stations, restaurants, hotels. Birds don't have as many options. For the sandhill crane, the main option has been latitude 41° north, longitude 98° west for millions of years, most likely because it's situated in the middle of the migratory route between wintering grounds in the south and breeding grounds in the north. Today we call that place the Platte River valley in the state of Nebraska.

The sandhill crane is one of the oldest species of birds on earth; some scientists put them at six million years old. The fossil of a close relative of the sandhill, the crowned crane, dating back ten million years, has been found in eastern Nebraska.

As the landscape transformed from savannah to what it is today, a river surrounded by corn, the sandhill cranes adapted along with it. The Platte River is around ten thousand years old, but it seems like the river and the cranes have been friends forever, they get along so well.

The cranes gather at the river every night by the thousands after spending their days in the surrounding cornfields. As the sun paints the sky blinding gold, then red, hundreds of thousands of cranes squawk, maneuver, jostle, and dance—a crane happy hour.

By last light, the cranes have settled for the night in the shallow water. The river weaves through large groups of sleeping cranes, protecting them with its built-in alarm sound of water splashing when a predator approaches, giving the cranes fair warning to flee.

It is at the cranes' morning rise and evening roost that the show for the humans transpires.

Show isn't the right word. But as I'm writing this piece, no other words seem up to the task. Some of the words we use to cover big moments—*awesome, amazing, extraordinary*—are so overused they've lost their luster. And they don't capture the feeling of joy that makes your cheeks ache from smiling and soothes your eyes with sun-warmed tears.

I was so stymied trying to describe the experience of the cranes, I almost gave up and put this piece on the shelf. But the idea of that didn't feel right.

The closest word that comes to describing the event of cranes is *numinous,* "having a strong religious or spiritual quality; indicating or suggesting the presence of a divinity."

My earthly point of entry into the world of cranes would be the Audubon's Rowe Sanctuary, where I would partake in morning and evening guided trips to view the cranes from observation blinds, wooden structures that let you watch birds without being seen.

The morning trip started early, dark and cold, a bracing twenty degrees: a reminder that March was still more lion than lamb. I arrived at the dimly lit Rowe Sanctuary Visitor Center and saw a small group gathered in a lighted room where the director of the center and knower of all-things-crane, Bill Taddicken, was preparing to guide us through a brief presentation.

With each incoming bit of information from the presentation, a concerning realization revealed itself: I didn't know the crane at all.

It wasn't a conscious decision not to delve into crane information before arriving. This had happened before when I'd visited birds—coming in totally cold. I'm not sure why I don't dig in and do some research on the bird I'm going to see—why I don't instigate the getting-to-know process before I'm actually about to see the bird.

A question I grapple with regarding birding (also life, come to think of it) is how to strike the balance between intellectually grasping ideas, facts, and data and experiencing the bird in a less intellectual way, through the emotions or instincts or whatever that part of us is that doesn't use words. When do I reach for the information? When do I put it aside?

It's important to be open, almost like a blank slate, upon experiencing the bird, but information can also help me find more meaning in what I'm seeing. Frans de Waal, the eminent primatologist, known for groundbreaking work on behavior and social intelligence of primates, says this about observing something you know nothing about: "Without pattern recognition, observation remains unfocused and random. It would be like watching a sport that you've never played and don't know much about. You basically see nothing." Perhaps the balance is to know some things about the thing you are observing and then pretend as if you don't know anything at all.

I was once on a bird outing with one of the most experienced ornithologists on seabirds, Steve Howell. Birders revere him; his book *Oceanic Birds of the World* is considered the bible on seabirds. He was leading a bird walk on land, and one of the participants saw a bird and declared, "Green jay." Steve, who was leading us, turned around and said, "How do you know?"

The green jay namer stammered, "Uh . . . because I just do . . ."

Steve said, "You're just naming it. Can you describe why it's a green jay?"

Not waiting for the guy's reply, Steve said, "Try not to just name the bird right away. Take it in as if you didn't know its name."

I was relieved that I wasn't the one who had blurted out "Green jay" and felt humbled because I am guilty of the very same thing—I just keep a lower profile. I was uncomfortable with my habit of quick naming and not getting to know what I'd named, but no one had pointed out as simply as Steve that you can pretend you don't know the thing.

Before we exited the Rowe Sanctuary Visitor Center to begin the walk to the blinds, we were split into three groups, correlative to the number of blinds. Each group was assigned a group leader. We would be led out single file. Once we exited the center, we were to remain absolutely silent. The cranes had to never know we were there.

The silence in my mind was punctuated by the sound of crunching snow beneath our feet. My face was cold. The situation was so heightened and foreign, I questioned my reality: Was this me, in Nebraska, walking with other humans in the dark to see a bird called a crane?

This was quite a level of commitment. You would think we

were on a special mission, sacrificing warmth and comfort for a noble cause. It might not be a mission, but it was special. And we were not an outlier or an isolated group of weirdos: thirty-five thousand visitors, spanning fifty countries, come every year from all over the world to view the cranes.

I saw shadows of the first group in our long line seamlessly veer off the path toward their blind. Soon another group slipped away. And then my group split off. I could not see, but that was fine. All I needed to do was follow. I entered a dark structure, like a long, narrow cabin, and because I was the first in line, I walked to the end. The other members filed in, stopping at whatever slat in the wall they landed at. The slats were not uniformly cut, nor were they at the same height; some were higher, some lower. I had to switch with the person next to me because my slat was too high and his was too low. We did this with gestures and whispers. Someone in the group forgot to whisper and blurted something out. They were immediately shushed. Someone dropped something. After a few moments of restless activity, we all found our personal world in front of our slat. It was pitch black and silent.

I'm not a meditator. I've tried off and on for thirty years.

As I stared out the narrow slat into nothingness, a restlessness stirred up meditation memories. I reminded myself that I didn't have to control my thoughts or pretend I was "letting go" when I really wasn't. My senses could experience the cold and wind, letting me know I was alive, albeit uncomfortable, and I didn't have to count or let that thought float by like a cloud. I could freely squirm in the tension of wanting to see the cranes right this minute, wanting to go back to bed, wishing I'd never come, then really wanting to see the cranes and blaming the sun for plodding along even though it was really the earth taking its slow sweet time.

With each degree of rotation, the dark unknown revealed itself: snow on land, scraggly shrubs poking out, a dark-gray mound appearing. Then a multiplicity of mounds emerged, transitioning slowly through shades of gray on the black water. Over time, the mounds shape-shifted into huddles of individual cranes. Slow-motion movement of wings adjusting, necks stretching. Muffled solo trumpet notes whispered out. Each degree of light brought more movement, sound, energy: huddles breaking open, cranes spreading out, regally striding past each other on articulated long legs.

The sun was rising in the sky. Light had announced itself, and so had the cranes. Everywhere was restless.

Loud. Swelling. Rising. Kinetic. All that energy crescendoed into cacophonous noise.

Individual cranes leapt five feet up—oiling the joints, getting ready, as if the ground was nudging them up. The individual cranes seemed to sense the whole, as if they were parts of a central nervous system that united under specific circumstances that only they knew.

An internal signal, heard by all, ignited by who knew what,

cued the congregation of cranes. En masse they lifted off. A crane volcano elegantly burst, filling the sky, raying out in all directions.

I tried to imprint the image in my mind, engrave the experience like an inner tattoo on my soul. I was buzzing with joy, delight, and tension. Was I equipped to capture this experience? I knew it was one of those once-in-a-lifetime experiences, so I exerted extra attention, almost pressuring my soul and senses to absorb every bit of it. And that pressure was uncomfortable; it constricted the receiving mechanism, making the experience a job, not a joy.

A similar doubt creeps in when I try to pray. I question: Am I doing it right? What am I supposed to hear? Who am I talking to anyway? It's a lack of trust in myself that lingers quietly below the surface, an old, unfriendly friend murmuring.

Birds are bigger than that murmur. If I focus on them, I am lifted, momentarily, out of the little mental ruts and confusions. I enter the zone where I don't think; I'm held by them, captivated by their existence. Eyes filled with salt drops, mouth agape, euphoric.

Ecstasy is exhausting.

I needed to rest up before sunset, when I would return for the evening show.

Come dusk, we trudged out the same way to the same blind, but it was all different. For one, it was light, and that made it, literally, the difference between night and day. I tried to recall the darkness from twelve hours ago, but it was nearly incomprehensible. Absolutely everything was different. I stood in front of the slat I had looked through in the early morning dark. The sky was pink, the snow was white.

I was still having trouble comprehending that this was the same place I'd seen that morning. But I liked thinking I knew a place and realizing I didn't know it at all, or rather, that I knew only a part of it. A place is not static, it changes through the day, through the seasons. Light, wind, water, clouds, animals, and the viewer affect it to varying degrees. Of course it wasn't the same place as this morning. Another major difference from the morning was that there were no cranes. They had been out eating all day, consuming the necessary fat for their long migration.

The group leader confirmed that cranes were departing the fields and would be here shortly. Birders have good intel.

I heard the cranes before I saw them, a faint chorus of honking in the distance.

And then in the sky, out of the pink, a massive, jagged circle of dots was born. The dots transformed into galumphing flying dinosaurs, homing in to spot number one, the Platte River. It looked like the helicopter scene from *Apocalypse Now,* the cranes an endless stream of bigger-than-life flying machines, but it wasn't scary or foreboding, it was a raucous, vibrant party. Hundreds of thousands of cranes were pouring into the Platte with ancient ease.

After an eternity, all the cranes, maybe all the sandhill cranes in the world, had landed in the Platte River.

It was a melee of squawking, honking, wing flapping, preening, facing off, backing away, attempting to bond, cementing a bond. Every crane was busy, not one was depressed and off alone. The setting sun did not tamp down the extravaganza. These cranes were like kids at a sleepover, unable to stop talking after being repeatedly told to quit it. They were silhouetted against pink, dark pink, red. Cranes and night became one. And then, they all fell silent.

12

Woodcock

The woodcock is a strange bird: a bit bigger than a robin, expertly cloaked in a rich palette of browns. If it is nestled on the ground among leaves, bark, needles, and twigs you'll have a hard time finding it. I've stared at a spot where there was solid confirmation of a woodcock but could not locate it. And I know I'm not alone.

When it stands up, the gorgeous brown hues can't quite compensate for the bird's oddness. It is out of proportion, drawn by an amateur: a stout body, large, round head, the eyes off scale, too far back and up too high, and the beak too long, like Pinocchio's nose.

The oddness is further exacerbated when it walks—or rather bobs, a kind of slow, bobble-head forward-and-back motion. It's surmised that this action of moving the feet back and forth gets the earthworms moving so they are easier to find.

But in the spring, at the stroke of dusk, the woodcock transforms into a kind of Cinderella when it takes to the night sky to perform a singular mating ritual known as a sky dance.

One day, as I was writing this chapter about the woodcock, I was interrupted by a woodcock—or rather, by someone mentioning a woodcock.

I was writing in one of my favorite cafés, % Arabica, in Brooklyn. Its floor-to-ceiling windows face the Brooklyn Bridge, the East River, and the Manhattan skyline. The café is a triple threat for me: it offers exhilarating views and excellent coffee made by friendly baristas, and it's right next to my local birding patch, Brooklyn Bridge Park. Sometimes I bird first and then stop for a coffee, or the other way around depending on mood, time, and weather. I stopped at the café at 5:00 p.m., the day before the winter solstice, to work on the woodcock chapter, the one you are reading now.

Right as I was finishing my writing session, I received a notification from my WhatsApp Brooklyn Bridge birding group. Birders that bird the same area, or patch, sometimes form chat groups to share intel on where the birds are. The message was from Doug Gochfeld, the master birder whom I counted birds with at the Tribute in Light. Doug and I keep finding our way to each other; we live in Brooklyn, so it's no surprise we both love Brooklyn Bridge Park.

His message read, *The woodcock was just out in the open, putting on a great show in the late gloaming between Long Pond and Mallow Pond.*

I looked up, and the crepuscular light heightened the liminal space I was floating in, reaffirming that I was in sync in my life, or at least with the woodcock.

I threw everything in my backpack and ran across Fulton Street toward Pier 1 between Long and Mallow Ponds.

But as I ran toward the pier, I realized I didn't know where Long or Mallow Pond was. I texted Doug and asked if he could help me. I made a mental note to learn the landmarks of the park; they are important waypoints for birders to find birds.

I wouldn't learn the names by looking at an official map. I would need to dive into local bird groups online, search for maps created by generous birders, and simply ask people. Birding landmarks remind me of Winnie-the-Pooh's map of the Hundred Acre Wood, which marked where the Woozle wasn't, where the six pine trees were, and where Eeyore's gloomy place was.

A few minutes passed with no text from Doug. I had never called Doug before and questioned whether our birding relationship allowed for a phone call. But birds trump social boundaries, so I called him. He was at the pilings, near Pier 3, counting seagulls. He said he would come to me, but I was impatient, so I started walk-running toward Pier 3.

We stayed on the phone as we made our way toward each other, him needing updates on my location because I was muddying the operation by not staying put.

Right as I heard him say, "I'm walking up the steps. Where are you?" I said, "At the top of the steps." We greeted each other mid-stairs.

Doug said, "Follow me. It's dark. Let's hope we can find him again."

We walked back up the steps and turned onto a narrow walkway that wove between corridors of thin woods to a spot overlooking a short slope, covered with leaves and natural detritus, leading down to a wet, marshy area between Mallow and Long Ponds. I knew this spot well but didn't know it had a name. I had watched a pair of juvenile black-crowned night herons grow up here over the summer. And in the fall, I had watched two Anna's hummingbirds feed on the nectar of jewelweed, less than a foot away.

Doug said this was the perfect spot for the woodcock. It was semi-wet and there were lots of leaves.

The chief horticulturist at Brooklyn Bridge Park, Paweł, had made sure that all the leaves were left. He's part of a growing environmental movement, Leave the Leaves. Not only do leaves provide nutrients to the microorganisms that are the life of the soil, but they also provide habitat for wildlife and insects. Even the Department of Agriculture supports it.

And I understand why. Leaving the leaves is better for the climate. All the leaves that are raked, bagged, and dumped in landfills amount to thirty-three million tons a year. Because there is no oxygen to break them down, the organic matter is released as methane, one of the major contributors to climate change.

Doug scanned the area with his binoculars. I stood by his side, in silent respect, while he scanned.

"I got him," he said.

I'm fascinated with how people describe what they are seeing and how to get you to see it. I always listen in when I hear a birder telling someone how to find a bird because I learn so much about how we see, how we describe what we see, and how difficult it is to be specific and universal at the same time. I've found it usually takes two or three attempts for the describer to get the seeker to the right spot. Usually, the description starts very general.

"It's there."

"Where is there?"

"You see that green thing? And that other green thing behind it? And then, you see that tree, the . . . well, that tree that's next to that bigger tree, anyway, there are like, leaves and things, and kind of a pile of leaves and to the right of that bunch of leaves is the bird, which is brown like the leaves."

Doug is a professional bird guide, so he's very skilled at helping other people see what he's seeing. But it still did take a couple of tries, though that says more about the woodcock's expert camouflage than it does about Doug's skills. Here is the one that got me to the woodcock.

"Okay, look at those two bushes right in front of us; from there follow the slope down to that branch jutting out horizontally. At the end of the branch and below it is a longish, light-green thing of grass, almost like a stalk. About six inches to the right of that large stalk of grass is what looks like a short, brown stump. That is the woodcock, but it has its head tucked in its wings so you can't see its face."

I had forgotten my binoculars, so Doug offered his. I zoomed into the world of the woodcock.

The air was cold. The ground was wet and cold. There had been a sprinkling of snow the other day. The park lights were bright. In the distance, the sound of a massive generator cut through with a mean white noise. It was dark where the woodcock was, but the park's bright lights glared almost everywhere else.

We heard the sound of two catbirds calling to each other, thinking it was still day. But it was night now and they should be asleep.

Doug thought the woodcock was wintering here. Someone had seen it yesterday and the day before that, and here he was again. If this spot worked, why not stay? If there was a lot of snow, he would be pushed somewhere else, perhaps. But woodcocks like wetlands and worms and grub in the leaf litter. It hit me that he was alone.

From the fall through the winter, woodcocks lead a solitary life. But for some reason, thinking of the woodcock all alone hit my heart more than imagining a lone red-tailed hawk. There are many birds that don't hang out in groups, and that fact generally doesn't make me feel sad. But maybe it's because the woodcock lives and sleeps on the ground, which makes it more vulnerable to predation. Maybe it's because it's up at night, when most other birds are asleep.

I'm a loner by nature and I love the night. I often find myself seeking out bird roosts in the fall and winter. During the heart of winter, at the end of the day, a large flock of robins near my home gather in a few large trees on Court Street. Before dusk, I like to stand across the street and watch them swoop one by one, sometimes in twos, into two tall bushes on the corner. There have been evenings, when walking on Court Street, that I stop in front of the dark bushes, thrilled with all the life stuffed in there.

The woodcock woke up. He cleaned and preened and fluttered up and down and then started digging his beak into the muck. One of the woodcock's many nicknames is *dig-face.* T. M. Rives, a guy I stumbled across on the internet who likes word origins, wanted to dig deeper into the meaning of *Scolopax,* the Latin name for woodcock, which means "woodcock." But he sensed there was something more going on, so he consulted another friend of his, a classicist, J. P. Bernbach, who dug a little deeper into the origin of the Greek word for the woodcock, *akalopas,* which translates to "skew-eyed" or "looking askance." Because woodcocks spend so much of their life with their beak in the dirt, the high placement of the eyes allows them to keep a lookout to the side, above, and even behind them.

They are more commonly known among birders by the name *timber doodle* or *dood.* But the name that struck my sympathy chord is a name the Seneca gave them, *God's leftovers*; God made them from the leftover parts of other birds.

I ALSO HAVE a special place in my heart for the woodcock because a woodcock once landed on my heart.

I was partying with a group of birders at the Biggest Week in American Birding Festival. Yes, birders party.

This guy, Jeff, announced, "It's woodcock time, let's go." Everyone grabbed their bins and went outside. I had no idea what we were doing, and I didn't care, because I knew it was going to be good.

We were in an area of rustic rental condos on the grounds of Maumee Bay State Park. We trekked over a parcel of the Maumee Bay State Park golf course and then gathered near some shrubs facing a slope leading to a flat grassy area. Everyone got down on their bellies, so I did too. With the triceps acting as a base, you can comfortably hold the bins to your eyes. Through the dusky light I made out a brown, medium-size bird bobbing. It fluttered a few feet off the ground and came back down. We stayed on our bellies, watching silently as a few more woodcocks appeared. Individual, kazoo-like notes dotted the spring air.

Jeff, the birder who had announced it was woodcock time, shouldered up next to me and whispered, "You hear that funny sound? That's called a *peent.* They do that before they're about to take off. Now, you see the woodcock standing apart from the others? Watch what he's about to do."

The woodcock spiraled up into the air, fluttering its wings, creating a strange whistling sound. At the apex, a moment of silence was followed by a repeated chirping, and then he zigzagged back down.

What the woodcock had just done is generally called a display, and more specifically a sky dance, an elaborate mating ritual performed every spring on what are called singing grounds. This nondescript grassy area was nothing when the woodcock wasn't there. It became a singing ground because the woodcock made it so.

Jeff said, "He's going to do that same thing again. When he starts to peent get ready. When he spirals up, run crouch style to where he took off and lie down on your back."

"Okay."

A ribbit of peents, then the liftoff. Jeff whispered, "Go."

I ran low to the ground like an Oompa Loompa, aiming for the spot whose exact location I was suddenly unsure of. I had no point of reference except for the woodcock, who was no longer there. Instead of following my mind, I let my feet stop me, flopping onto my back. The woodcock was up somewhere above me, fluttering, whistling. Then suspended silence, broken by chirping. More fluttering sounds, reminding me of old-fashioned toy planes made from balsa wood and a rubber band. Then the woodcock appeared, helicoptering straight down to me and landing on my chest.

My world narrowed and widened simultaneously, as if I had entered a new dimension but in a sacred bubble made up of me and this living, breathing, feathered entity. There was a woodcock on my chest and I felt light. The exaltation brought awareness to the old stuff weighing me down, detritus like the leaves whose natural process of breaking down had been thwarted by fear and time. I didn't want to keep holding back, saying no, reliving old hurts.

This woodcock was giving it his all, because that's what you do. The unspoken mandate while we're all here: keep moving toward life, not away from it.

I slowly moved my eyes in his direction without moving my head. His focus on finding a mate was so paramount, he paid me no notice; I was just a patch of grass to him. I tried not to look at him directly because it didn't feel right, almost as if I would be intruding on some sacred rite. It was an honor to have him on my chest. I didn't want to use him as some party trick. He was working his ass off to find a mate, doing his part to ensure that his odd species continued on.

He peented, then hopped off my chest. I gently turned my head in his direction and watched him strut-wobble into the dark.

When I heard the weird whistling sound I sprinted back to my tribe, inhaling the smell of the earth, pungent with spring, ready to burst. As I reached the group, I was tempted to slide, as if coming into home base, but plopped down instead. Jeff, my birder coach, welcomed me back. He put up his palm and I high-fived him.

I lay on my stomach, resting my chin on my hands. I was gushing with joy and trying to contain it. If I could, I would race around in wide circles like a happy dog. For now, all that energy was in my face, my body. I could privately sneak a crazy smile; it was dark, no one could see me, but I felt seen.

13

Godspeed

It is May 13, and the sun is about to set, with winds swirling up from the south. At home in Brooklyn, I think birds might be on the move.

I check BirdCast, whose homepage claims: "Bird Migration Forecasts in Real-Time." The first entry states, "Migration Alert: Northeastern North American floodgates open May 13th." Underneath is a NEXRAD (Next Generation Radar) weather map of the United States on a black background.

The map view shows only outlines of states and borders, a transparent country. Instead of names and places I see splotchy puffs of electric cerulean blue. I click the image, and it animates the cerulean puffs, which slow-motion burst into a bloom of cobalt. That burst is birds.

The individual blooms of cobalt blue coalesce within five seconds into one body of blue. East of the Mississippi, from the South to the North, hundreds of thousands of birds are taking off at once, one half hour after sunset. Governed by a mysterious rhythm, they take flight synchronously.

Watching the burst of blue, I burst with joy and race to grab my bins, my light down jacket, a windbreaker, my iPhone, wallet, keys. I bound down the stairs out of my building, skitter to the corner of Clinton Street and Kane, and search the horizon for a cab. One emerges in the distance, and I shoot my arm up; that's my cab.

As I hop in, I say, "Empire State Building, please." The cabbie says, "Empire State? At night?"

"Yes, at night."

The cab moves through the tree-lined streets toward Atlantic Avenue.

"Huh. Most people go there during the day. Why go at night? What are you gonna see?"

"Birds!"

"Birds?"

"Yes!"

We merge onto the BQE. The cab sails over the highway's concrete curve, and there she is: the Empire State, her spire a beacon. With my mind's eye, I zoom out wide to get a side perspective. I see myself in the cab and birds high in the sky, directly above me, all of us propelling forward. Motorcades thrill me, and I'm nestled in one that's a thousand strong, timeless—a force-of-migration motorcade.

I revel in the absolute fact that I know birds are in the sky, directly above me. Sometimes I experience this feeling as a wish, but it's not a wish right now; I know it for certain. I saw it with my own two eyes on the radar. *I saw you taking off. We are united, with you above and me below, while the cabbie takes me closer to you.*

We pull up in front of the Empire State Building. I dash out of the cab and push through the glass doors. Before me is a long hallway and a quarter block of stanchions and rope snaking toward the distant ticket counter. No one is waiting in line, but I'm still required to navigate the snaking ropes. I want to run, to cry out in exaltation as I prepare to launch up to the sky. But if I run, I'm out; guards line the place. I subtly increase my pace from a step to a slide across the floor, polished and smooth. I'm skating, gliding my way to the ticket counter. The guards eye me but don't make a move; maybe the grin on my face disarms them.

I'm in the elevator going up, up, up. A couple stands with me, and a small group of tourists from somewhere in Europe. We're escorted out of the long-ride elevator down a narrow hallway to another elevator. Up again, and up. Stop.

We emerge just outside of a room enclosed by glass, surrounded by sky. I push open the doors into the glass room and rush to another door off to the side that leads to the outer deck. I test the deck door—nothing, it doesn't budge as the wind pushes against the other side. The couple from the elevator joins me at the door and throw their weight against it too. We nudge it open a crack and the wind heaves it back. Giggles spurt forth—a confused joy at facing a force that is bigger and stronger but not threatening. We push harder and are heaved back once again. And again.

I imagine a 0.5-ounce blackpoll warbler flying through this wind.

We begin to push; the door swooshes open and we tumble onto the deck.

Wind. It's all that exists. Wind in my eyes, my ears, my mind, my spine. I gently move forward to test its strength and it presses me back. Wind wins. I'm laughing but I have respect for it. You got me. You are stronger than me. And I love it.

I look up. A stream of birds above me. I'm facing south to greet them as they arrive, and they all look straight ahead to the north, steady and true. Wings beat measuredly on the wind, a procession of all shapes and sizes. I hear chips, squawks, peeps. I scan the sky, and everywhere, to the east and west; it is filled with birds streaming from the south. I turn my head and follow the flow to the north, and then, like a typewriter carriage, return my gaze to the south.

I could be like Rumi and let the rhythmic beating of the wings twirl my body around in a circle, one arm lifted to the sky and the other dropped to the earth. I'm in perfect balance, beaming at the birds with my own personal radar that reflects them back to me. It causes teardrops to stream down my face.

I want to bow to them. I want to hand each one a medal. I would drape one around each of their necks and say, "You are receiving this medal for your grit, your determination, your will to live. You will land somewhere. Do you even know where? How do you know if it's the right spot? What if there's no food? You will keep flying." The champion long-distance traveler of the bird kingdom, a female marbled godwit named E7, holds the record for distance flown: 7,258 miles, nonstop.

But most of them will land come morning. For some it will be a stopover, for others it will be home. If it's home, they'll fight for a spot to live, then find a mate of the opposite sex.

They will copulate and raise a brood, and another brood, maybe a third if they're lucky. They've made life. They risked their life migrating to make life.

I tilt my head down from the sky to the earth. The humans around me are all looking down. There's a wonderland above us, but they haven't heard the good news. They're pressed against the protective fences lining the perimeter of the outer deck, gazing down below, a bird's-eye view on our city, its bright lights pulsing, sparkling, shimmering. I join my fellow humans. I look down for the first time since arriving at the deck. I can't see them, but I know they are down below, moving inexorably forward on their own paths. Living.

I lift my eyes again, focus them up and out into the northern distance. I watch birds stream toward the vanishing point on the horizon and am filled with ecstasy and desire and sorrow. Sometimes I don't want to live, or I don't know how to live, or don't know why. These migrating birds don't ask why. They're moved by the force of life, and I'm moved by them. One can only recognize something if they know it already; "recognizing" is knowing it again.

If I'm recognizing the life force in birds, then wouldn't that mean . . .

"Yes." Some interior part of me speaks with conviction to the rest of myself. "Don't you see? You wouldn't recognize this life force if you didn't know it already, know it deep in your being. The birds are only reflecting back to you what you understand and hold within."

My fellow humans on the deck are moving inside. The guards call out: five minutes until closing.

I look up once more before I return to earth. I focus hard, willing my mind to etch this moment into a vivid memory. But then I think, don't worry about the memory. Just enjoy it right now.

And I whisper, "Thank you, birds."

Godspeed.

Afterword

I said at the beginning of the book that I wanted to share my reports of this endless living world with you, my kindred spirits. As I've visited bookstores, festivals, and events with *Turning to Birds,* I've enjoyed receiving your reports as well. Here is a report from a friend that gets to the essence of what I hoped the book might inspire:

> *I confess, I've never been a bird noticer. Until now. It's like this whole invisible world—invisible to me, anyway—is suddenly visible. I'm starting to notice. I stop and look now.*

If I had any doubts that we are hardwired to respond to the natural world, they have been put to rest by the stories, just like this one, that readers have shared with me. Meanwhile, I have continued creating new reports, too, and I have one more that I would like to share with you.

Recently, I ran into two birder friends in Manhattan who were on their way to locate a saltmarsh sparrow; there had been a rare sighting of one. They invited me to join them, but I fell back into my automatic reaction of "no." I assumed I had already seen one, and as you now know, I have a complicated relationship with sparrows.

Fifteen minutes later, as I sat in a café, sipping my coffee and feeling lonely, I heard a whisper in my head: *Do you even know what the saltmarsh sparrow is?* I went to Cornell's Lab of Ornithology website to find out.

The first line said, "Saltmarsh Sparrows are flashes of color hidden in the brown expanses of tidal saltmarshes, their only home."

And then I read, "Saltmarsh Sparrow is in very real danger of extinction within the next few decades due to its small population size, declining trend, and the reality of rising sea levels."

It was now clear to me that I had actually never seen one and didn't know the bird at all.

I rushed to the address my friends had shared with me: Borough of Manhattan Community College on Chambers Street and the West Side Highway in Lower Manhattan. I made my way to the shared location point within the brutalist concrete structure. I arrived at an odd-shaped courtyard, half the size of a basketball court. On one side stood a wall of dirty floor-to-ceiling reflective glass, and on the other side, a two-foot-high brick retaining wall with plantings terraced up a short slope. My two friends, along with five other birders, binoculars to their eyes, were all focused on an area in the plantings. I looked where they looked and spotted the small sparrow with a stripe of soft golden orange above the eye and one on the chin.

In silence, we watched the bird make its way through the plantings, pecking at the ground, pecking at the leaves. The plants were all native, housing seeds and insects that the sparrow had evolved with over millennia. A familiar, nutritious meal.

We watched for at least a half hour, a long time to watch a bird in one area. Birds get around; they fly, they're busy, and it's not safe for them to stay in one spot too long. But migratory birds are tired and hungry. It takes time to fuel up, and clearly this bird had no reserves.

My friend Doug said it was probably on its way to a coastal area further south. This little strip of native plants, in this strange concrete area, helped it survive another day.

The bird flew from the plantings to the middle of the courtyard. My throat got tight and my eyes stung as I watched this bird that lives solely in tidal saltmarshes make its way in a concrete land with no salt, marsh, or water nearby.

Every bird counts, but it was striking how this one seemed to count more. Perhaps it's because when a count gets lower, the end becomes clearer.

This individual saltmarsh sparrow living one more day means its species survives one more day. And even though its species will most likely be the next North American one to go extinct, this bird keeps on striving. Carpe diem—make the most of the day.

Acknowledgments

This book's trajectory reminds me of a ball in a Rube Goldberg machine; each action triggering the initiation of the next one.

Michael Male said, "Why don't you write your own thing. I'll read your pages."

Ada Calhoun said, over and over, "I love it!"

Lisa Dwan said, "I adore you," over and over, and I believed it.

Annie Schmidt said, "I'd love to help, let me see what I can do," and brought me to Mia.

Mia Walker shined her bright light on me and still does. "It's a love letter," she said.

Marie Howe said, "I'm with you, Lili," and I felt it.

Jason Weinberg said, "I'm not sure what it is, but I have someone you should meet," and he brought me to David.

David Kuhn said, "Lovely. Why don't you write about one bird, any bird you've seen, and email it to me."

Nate Muscato said assuredly, "Just keep doing what you're doing."

And I kept their loving belief alongside me the whole time.

Maria Popova offered support as well as valuable insights for the cranes chapter.

Tara Mohr helped me play it big.

Imogen Poots declared her belief in me with her bright blue eyes. And I got it.

Crown said, "We'd love to have you." And they meant it.

Before I set out for my maiden voyage, I asked my editor—Libby Burton—if there was one piece of advice she could send me off with, and she said, "Think about what you're gifting the reader." Libby gifted me and guided me throughout the process. I always knew she was with me. Matt Inman graciously picked up the baton, guiding me to the finish line with love.

I need to also acknowledge a few people whom I don't know and do not know me, but their influence was profound:

Cal Newport taught me about Deep Work.

Verlyn Klinkenborg taught me to penetrate the sentence.

George Saunders taught me to read what I wrote the day before and if there's a "meh," dig in till it's no longer "meh." One "meh" at a time.

The Center for Fiction Writers Studio—my writing haven. Also havens: % Arabica and Amano Café. And to all the kick-ass baristas who've poured me my cup of joy.

Finally:

Queen Maeve, my everything. Nick, husband, partner, collaborator, also my everything. They wrap their arms around me and lift me up while keeping me grounded.

About the Author

LILI TAYLOR is an award-winning movie, television, and theater actor. In the birding world, Taylor is a board member of the National Audubon Society and New York City Bird Alliance. She nests in Brooklyn and upstate New York with her husband, the memoirist and poet Nick Flynn, and their daughter.